The Sfas Emes Anthology

The Joy of Sukkos

❖

*A Presentation of the Thoughts and Insights
of the Sfas Emes
regarding the Achievement of Joy through
the Celebration of Sukkos*

RABBI MOSHE APTER

P·U·B·L·I·S·H·E·R·S

New York · London · Jerusalem

Published and distributed
in the U.S., Canada and overseas by
C.I.S. Publishers and Distributors
180 Park Avenue, Lakewood, New Jersey 08701
(908) 905-3000 Fax: (908) 367-6666

Distributed in Israel by
C.I.S. International (Israel)
Rechov Mishkalov 18
Har Nof, Jerusalem
Tel: 02-518-935

Distributed in the U.K. and Europe by
C.I.S. International (U.K.)
89 Craven Park Road
London N15 6AH, England
Tel: 81-809-3723

Book and cover design: Deenee Cohen
Typography: Devorah Rozsansky

ISBN 1-56062-165-6 hard cover
1-56062-181-8 soft cover
Library of Congress Catalog Card Number
92-73913

PRINTED IN THE UNITED STATES OF AMERICA

Printed by MORIAH OFFSET CO. 718—693-3800

TABLE OF CONTENTS

❖

FOREWORD

❖

BY RABBI ARYEH KAPLAN ZAL

There are two seven-day festivals in the Jewish year—
Pesach and *Sukkos*. Since seven days is the measure of
creation, both of these festivals have the connotation of
creation, so to speak, of our creating something new in
ourselves. On *Pesach*, we create a new *internal* environment
for ourselves—inside our bodies—by eating *matzah* and food
that is kosher for *Pesach*. On *Sukkos*, we create a new *external*
environment for ourselves—through sitting and eating in
the *sukkah*, and through waving the *lulav* to all six directions.

The connotation of *Sukkos* is, therefore, that of our
influence on the external world. Before the Torah was
given, G-d told the Israelites that they would be a kingdom
of priests and a holy nation. As the Seforno explains, a
kingdom of priests means that we will teach the non-Jewish
world about G-d. This is the message of *Sukkos* when seventy
bullocks were sacrificed for the seventy nations of the

9

world. The Talmud also says that in the Messianic age the nations of the world will be tested through the *sukkah*. *Pesach*, on the other hand, teaches us how to develop our own internal relationship with G-d, which involves our other mission of being a holy nation.

In this book on *Sukkos*, Rabbi Moshe Apter brings the teachings of the Sfas Emes, one of the most profound of all modern Jewish thinkers, to the English-speaking world. For, of course, the message of *Sukkos* is not primarily for the nations of the world, but for all those who are alienated from Torah and *mitzvos*, especially our youth today, who are like infants captured among the gentiles.

All alienation ultimately stems from Adam's sin—which involved a tree. Therefore, on *Sukkos*, we take four species of tree to rectify this sin. After we have prayed for forgiveness on *Yom Kippur*, we can do our part to rectify Adam's sin that affected all mankind. We wave these four species in all directions to rectify the effects of sin in all corners of the globe.

As always, Rabbi Apter has done an excellent job in rendering these profound teachings into English. May this work have the effect of bringing those who read it closer to Torah and *mitzvos*—in all corners of the globe.

Aryeh Kaplan

INTRODUCTION

---❖---

A psalm for the thank offering: Make a joyful noise to God all the lands! Serve God with gladness! Come into His presence with singing! Know that God is the Lord. It is He that made us, and we are His; we are His people, the sheep of His pasture. Enter His gates with thanksgiving and His court with praise! Give thanks to Him, bless His name! For God is good; His steadfast love endures for ever, and His faithfulness to all generations.

(Tehillim 100:1-5)

Our holidays are a time of joy and gladness. Joy in being with our family, friends and our people. Joy in reaping the fruits of our labor in the land of Israel, and joy in our well being. Joy in the uplifting of our hearts that sends our spirits soaring. The one holiday which emphasizes this joy to the utmost in *Sukkos*, as it is written, You should rejoice in your holiday, and you should be only joyous. (*Devarim* 16:14) This joyous holiday should leave its mark on us for the rest of the year; it teaches us that there is joy in the world, a joy can be found.

This teaching is true despite all appearances to the contrary. Whoever opens his eyes sees a world with suffering, death and misery in great abundance. Not only is there much apparent suffering, but even our joys are impermanent. Joys come and go, and we cannot seem to get a good hold on them. They slip through our fingers as sand with but few grains remaining. People grope in darkness seeking joy of the body and of the spirit, only to find illusion.

Rabbi Nachman of Breslav, a giant among *chassidic* masters, once said, "The World-to-Come, the perfect world, we at least believe in. But this material world, the here and now, how can anyone believe in it? The only thing to do is run to the refuge of God."

True joy is the product of harmony when every facet of our life is in harmony and rooted in God. Then we are able to make contact with the world of essence, the divine, infinite and lasting reality. This rootedness we find in the commandment of *sukkah*.

There was once a time when *Sukkos* was a nearly invisible holiday in America, when there was little visible sign of the holiday on the American streets. If at all, it was only at the synagogue or temple that one could eat in the *sukkah*. To some Jews, *Sukkos* was apparently too brazen a sign of Jewishness. How embarrassing to have neighbors watch the construction of a temporary hut in the modern age of the twentieth century in the city? What for? Even today there are "embarrassed" Jews who do not enjoy the depth and meaning of the Torah way of life. Yet, *Sukkos* is no longer invisible. American Jews are filled with a new courage and pride in their heritage and traditions. The Torah, too, is brighter for them as they watch the world at large slipping into an abysmal darkness, a darkness of aimless groping and insecurity. The Torah way is increasingly popular.

One can now walk through Jewish neighborhoods in many parts of the world and see the *sukkah*; the sight of grownups and children walking to the synagogues with the *esrog* and *lulav* is no longer uncommon. It is beautiful to take part in one's traditions, to rejoice with family and friends, to feel pride in one's people. With pride must come a deeper understanding of the true essence of the holiday of *Sukkos*. What strengths do we gather from the *sukkah* and the four plant species? We must learn how the holiday elevates each one of us by its absolute escape from the world of illusion and "running to the refuge of God."

The *chassidic* masters have taught that each time one does a *mitzvah* it should be done as if for the very first time. We should not say, "Oh, *Sukkos*? That's what we did last year!" The *sukkah* of this year should be totally new and elevated compared to last year's.

How can we accomplish this? By learning and relearning the significance of this joyful holiday. Thus, when one is ready to learn, one chooses the very best teachers. Among these are the *chassidic* masters who have revealed, illuminated and clarified the deep secrets and symbolism of the Torah. Based on Kabbalah, which contains the innermost secrets of our relationship with God, the Creation and the meaning of Torah verses, the teachings of the *chassidic* masters elucidate the most profound concepts, using comparisons, analogies and parables so that even the uninitiated person can understand it.

Chassidic teachings touch not only the mind but also the emotions. Therefore, they relate to one's personal life and existential struggles.

13

The Sfas Emes Anthology is a presentation of the luminous thoughts of the *chassidic* master Rabbi Yehudah Aryeh Leib Alter, the second leader of the *chassidic* dynasty of Gur, the son of the first Rebbe of Gur and the grandson of the Chidushei Harim. Orphaned as a young boy, he was educated by his grandfather who was one of the greatest Torah sages of that time. Even at that young age, he learned Torah with great diligence, eighteen hours a day. To visiting scholars, his grandfather would say, "Look at how my grandson studies Torah!" In 1870, at the age of twenty—three, he became Rebbe of Gur. He molded Gur as a center of *chassidus*, attracting tens of thousands of followers from all over Europe. His commentaries on the Talmud made him renowned as a great Torah scholar as well as a brilliant leader. For more than thirty years he counseled his followers to live with fervent devotion to the Torah, both in study and deed. In 1905, a few days before he passed away, he wrote the last of his written words, Lips of truth (*sfas emes*) stand firm forever. (*Mishlei* 12:19) And because they were the last words of his earthly sojourn, his sons chose them as a lasting tribute and named all his writings *Sfas Emes*.

The *Sfas Emes* on the Torah, which is the basis for this book, has a singularly deep and exciting approach to interpreting its verses and topics. Besides its depth, it encompasses a wide spectrum of quotations, analogies and comparisons from the Talmud, *Midrash* and *Zohar*. His teachings are constantly bursting with new ideas in every sentence, phrase and word. He is like a brook, endlessly bubbling forth new ideas that taste different each time one drinks from it. Yet the very richness of the teachings, the endless facets and nuances make it extremely difficult to encapsulate and convey them.

Some fifteen years ago, while using the teachings of the Sfas Emes as the basis for holiday seminars, I decided to focus on central ideas and clarify them by explanation and parables. After a time, we discovered themes and patterns. We compared and contrasted, until the approach of the Sfas Emes was slowly discovered. This book represents what we had understood of his commentary; our learning, our struggle to comprehend and explain. No doubt, it is not the only interpretation, and most certainly there will be differing opinions as to what the Sfas Emes actually meant. This book is my understanding of the Sfas Emes. It is not a straight translation but rather an approximation, carefully elaborated and elucidated by the judicious addition of parables. A list of sources appears as an appendix to the book and the reader is invited to retrace my steps and make his own comparison and judgment.

In giving the book a form more akin to its original *chassidic* flavor, we have used the Hebrew for names and references. And for those who are more familiar with the English form, the glossary includes a complete list of the English translation of all of them.

From this book, I pray the reader will acquire a taste of the deeper significance of *Sukkos* by learning to abandon falsehood and illusion to find peace in God's refuge. By fully participating in *Sukkos*, you will be granted true and lasting joy. You will find the roots of your soul as you bask in God's protection. You will unite as one with your people and live with their collective strength. You will find a joy that will sustain you not only during *Sukkos* but year round.

I am very grateful to a number of people who have been of great help to me in completing this project. I would like to thank my wife and children for their patience and encouragement. The talented staff of C.I.S. Publishers has been extremely helpful, and I would like to give specific thanks to Rabbi Avraham Marmorstein, my distinguished editor, to Art Director Deenee Cohen, who designed this book, and to the typographer Devorah Rozsansky who produced it. Last and most important, we are thankful to our Creator, who gives us our very life and sustains us always. May He continue to strengthen the light of the Torah among us, and with it light up all the corners of the globe, and help us experience the holiday of *Sukkos* as the ultimate refuge for all of Israel. Amen.

Moshe Apter
Elul, 5752

The Joy of Sukkos

A Presentation of the Thoughts and Insights
of the Sfas Emes
regarding the Achievement of Joy through
the Celebration of Sukkos

1

THE TIME OF OUR REJOICING

You shall keep the feast of Sukkos seven days, when you make your ingathering from your threshing floor and your wine presses; you shall rejoice in your holiday, you and your son and your daughter, your manservant and maid-servant, the Levite, the sojourner, the fatherless and the widow who are within your towns. For seven days you shall keep the feast to Hashem your Lord at the place which Hashem will choose; because Hashem your Lord will bless you in all your produce and in all the work of your hands, so that you will be altogether joyful.

(Devarim 16:13-15)

There is great awe and fear during *Rosh Hashanah* and *Yom Kippur*, and it is followed by a great rejoicing during *Sukkos*. We can compare this to a king who prepared a banquet for his family and attendants. The banquet was ready, and the king entered. All were filled with great awe and fear, and they stood motionless. After the formal greetings, the guests sat down to eat. Those who were intimately friendly with the king relaxed and talked with him. They talked and joked and enjoyed his company. Those who were mere servants remained respectfully quiet during the entire meal.

When we are filled with awe and fear on *Yom Kippur*, it seems as if we are strangers to Hashem and as if we are afraid of Him. When we rejoice on *Sukkos*, however, it becomes clear that our awe and fear of Hashem is from our closeness to Him.

Similarly, Avraham named his son Yitzchak, whose name means laughter. Yitzchak? Is he not the most severe of the three forefathers—referred to by his own son as the "fear of Yitzchak"? Why should he be called laughter? Because his awareness of the stern judgment of Hashem brought him great joy.

When Avraham was about to offer Yitzchak as a sacrifice to Hashem, he was stopped by a voice from Heaven. Instead, he found a ram tangled by its horn in the thicket. The ram's horn is used on *Rosh Hashanah* to make the sound of awe and fear, but the inner content is laughter. The laughter of Hashem as He sees the awe and respect of His people. This inner laughter of *Rosh Hashanah* is concealed until the holiday of *Sukkos*. Then it can be revealed. For by then we have no terror, no specter of retribution hangs over our heads. But we are awed by Hashem's greatness. We show the outer awe on *Rosh Hashanah* and the inner laughter on *Sukkos*.

❖

*E*ach *Rosh Hashanah*, the creation receives new vitality and resilience. On a deeper level, the world is constantly being created and renewed. This constant creation is revealed at special times during the year.

Each time the world is created anew, there is a renewal of Hashem's selection processes. The ideal path, ideal teachings and teachers are pronounced once again with a fresh edict from Hashem. On *Rosh Hashanah*, the Jewish people, who are concealed among all the nations of the world, are judged. Now after this judgment, they are pronounced as chosen, set aside and placed in the *sukkah*—the earthly representation of Hashem's presence.

Sukkos is the rejoicing of the Jewish people at being reinvested with the status of a chosen people.

—————————— ❖ ——————————

*H*ashem's honor will be forever and Hashem will be happy with His work. (*Tehillim* 104:31)

True happiness is present when Hashem's Name is completely revealed in the world. Such revelations will not happen until the nature of the world changes from deception and illusion. Revelation is light, for it is written, The light is planted for the righteous; it is planted and concealed in the earth at present, but for the straight of heart, there is joy. (*Tehillim* 97:11) To be straight without illusion or deception belongs to a future Messianic era.

However, a person who has performed *teshuvah*, who has repented, can transport himself into that future era. As part of the *teshuvah* process, he has transformed time into the infinite by restoring his past and revitalizing his future. He has caught a glimpse of the path leading directly to the Throne of Honor, the Divine Essence. In that place there is true happiness.

Therefore, after the repentance of *Yom Kippur*, we are transported to an island of a world-to-come where we find true happiness and great rejoicing. The *sukkah* is that island, an enclave of the world-to-come.

❖

*T*he *sukkah* reminds us of the Beis Hamikdash. In the days of old, all the Jews would leave their homes and journey to its courtyard. So, too, all Jews leave their homes and go to the *sukkah*.

Whenever we are reminded of the Beis Hamikdash we cannot help but be happy. As it is written, I was happy when I was told, "Let us go to the house of Hashem." (*Tehillim* 122:1) People would say to King David, When is this old fellow going to die so that we can start building the Beis Hamikdash? (*Makos* 10a) David knew that the Beis Hamikdash would be built only after his death. Still, he was happy to hear people yearning for its construction. Moreover, David continues, Jerusalem, built as a city which is bound firmly together. The hearts of all of Israel are bound together in this city of Jerusalem. Similarly, in the *sukkah* every Jew can find his place. Therefore, as soon as one hears that one is going to the *sukkah*, a living symbol of the Beis Hamikdash, one immediately rejoices and is glad of heart.

❖

*T*he Torah mentions joy during the holiday of *Sukkos*. You should rejoice in your holiday, and you should be only joyous. (*Devarim* 16:14) And you shall rejoice before Hashem your Lord seven days. (*Vayikra* 23:40)

Why is *Sukkos* especially suited for joy?

Joy is the product of harmony. On a small scale, when

each member cell of an organ supports the life of the other cells, then there is joy. When all the organs give life and vitality to each other, there is joy for the whole being. However, if health, vitality and life cannot be transmitted from one organ to another, there is instead loss, yearning and pain. The breaking of the links among the various parts shatters the harmony and results in sadness.

This is also true for mankind as a whole. The purpose of creating human beings was that they might reveal truth in the universe, which is that Hashem is the Master, and nature is divine.

The divine nature of the world is in exile and hiding until man redeems it. How does he redeem it? By dealing with it in a divine manner. Each item which is thus redeemed becomes part of the redeemed universe, part of the harmony and joy of being.

Hashem wants all the nations of the world to be part of this harmony and joy. As it is written, Hashem desires for the sake of His righteousness. (*Yeshayahu* 42:21) He wants all the nations to share in the righteousness, but they refuse.

The task of the Jewish nation is to transform the world so that all mankind participates in its harmony and joy. In order to do this, the Jewish people needed to be prepared in stages. First they needed to be separated from all erroneous paths. This was accomplished with the exodus from Egypt, which severed them from idol worship and the abominations of Egypt. When they received the Torah at Mount Sinai, they were further separated from erroneous paths of the other nations. Therefore, the holidays which commemorate these events, *Pesach* and *Shavuos*, lack the fullness of harmony and joy. Not only are the other nations not included, on the contrary, they are excluded. However, with the holiday of *Sukkos* finally comes a taste of true joy. The Jewish people make offerings for all the seventy nations and bring harmony to all of mankind.

Similarly, the Jewish nation shares three names with their ancestor Yaakov: Yaakov, Yisrael and Yeshurun. Yaakov is the one who runs away from his brother Esav and chooses instead the godly way. This corresponds to *Pesach*, for the humble nation runs away from the arrogant one. Yisrael contains the two Hebrew words, *Li Rosh*, meaning, I have a head. The head is wisdom—the wisdom of the Torah; therefore, this name represents *Shavuos*. Finally, Yeshurun means not merely straight, but making straight, referring to the work of the Jewish nation. They make all of mankind and the entire creation straight. This last name corresponds to *Sukkos*. Thus, harmony is at its peak during *Sukkos*, and it is accompanied with great joy.

Let us also participate in the work of redeeming the world, bringing with it joy to all of mankind.

——————— ❖ ———————

*G*o eat your bread with enjoyment, and drink your wine with a merry heart, for Hashem has already approved what you do. (*Koheles* 9:7)

The Jewish people are connected to the divine roots of the world. When they sin, there is separation from these roots; the world feels to them like chaos. When they repent, however, their connection to the divine roots becomes clear again; and all is restored to its proper place.

The root of all souls is in the throne of Hashem's glory, *Kiseh Hakavod*. Therefore, our sages have taught, Repentance is so great that it reaches to the Throne of Honor. (*Yoma* 8a) Similarly, the image of Yaakov's face, the sum of all Jewish souls, is carved into Hashem's throne.

By repenting on *Yom Kippur*, each of our souls finds its original place in Hashem's throne. Everything is restored to its proper order and it is written, for Hashem has already approved. Everything is approved retroactively as if it were in its original order. *Sukkos* is when we rejoice for the restoration of all which appeared out of place. The great joy comes from realizing that it was really in order all of the time.

❖

*A*s the apple tree among the trees of the forest . . . for in his shade I have yearned to be. (*Shir Hashirim* 2:3)

Of all the trees of the forest, it is the apple tree to which the shelter of Hashem's protection is compared. The apple tree gives little shade, and very few turn to it as a refuge from the sun. Similarly, the path of divine illumination was rejected by the arrogant nations who did not see it as sufficiently beneficial to them; only the Jewish nation yearned to be in His shade and ignored the hardships. They walked with Moshe into the desert, from slavery to Hashem's shelter, and they yearned to remain forever.

So great was the joy of being under the shelter of Hashem's clouds of glory that the Jewish people longed to remain forever in His protective Presence. This yearning was rewarded with the *mitzvah* of *sukkah*, a shelter for those who seek Hashem. Joy is there in abundance for anyone seeking the divine shelter.

❖

*T*he ideal place for man on earth was Gan Eden, the Garden of Eden. This was the most harmonious spot and state of being. Unfortunately, mankind was expelled from this ideal state and sent into exile to survive by the sweat of his brow. Still, on special occasions, special places and spiritual levels, we catch a glimpse of the Gan Eden. One such place is the *sukkah*; therefore, it is a source of joy and boundless rejoicing.

❖

*T*he human soul is not from this physical world, it is an alien being imported from the divine realm. The light of our souls shines through the dark and obscure nature of this world and leads us to the right path. Thus, we are guided and enlightened by the power of our soul. If we err and sin, however, the concealment of the world makes the truth more obscure, and the light of our soul no longer has the power to guide us.

If we subsequently perform *teshuvah*, if we repent and return to Hashem, the soul is restored to its former strength and shines through the darkness of the apparent world. Once again, it gives light for our life and guides us to the correct path of Hashem.

Each one of us has two sources of positive energy untouched and unharmed by even the worst sins. There is a kernel of absolute holiness in each of us which is forever pure. This energy is called *tzaddik*, the righteous one. The other is an energy in each of us which seeks home, the Throne, Hashem's glory. This energy is called *baal teshuvah*, the repentant one.

When we return to Hashem on *Yom Kippur*, both of these energies shine within us, through us and for us. We feel their strength on *Sukkos* when we run to the shelter of Hashem. Our happiness and joy knows no bounds; we are whole and alive once more.

2

THAT YOUR GENERATIONS
SHALL KNOW

*In booths you shall dwell for seven days; all that
are native in Israel shall dwell in booths, so that
your generations may know that I caused the people
of Israel to dwell in booths when I brought them out
of the land of Egypt; I am Hashem your Lord.*

(Vayikra 23:42-43)

When a man meets a woman and chooses her to be his
wife, he then takes her to his house which is symbolized by the *chuppah*. Thus, too, did Hashem choose the
Jewish people in the Egyptian exodus and then take them to
His house—the *sukkah*.

A shepherd quickly gathers his belongings and runs to the
shed when the rain begins to fall. He takes only his most
treasured personal belongings and leaves the rest outside.
Thus, too, did Hashem gather his treasured personal

possession, the people of Israel, and bring them into the
sukkah, leaving all seventy nations outside.

Why did Hashem choose to teach His path, His law and
His wisdom to such a small part of mankind? Would it not
have been better to share them with all of mankind?

The truth is that the Jewish people among the nations is
like a soul inside a body. The soul is the pure vitality and
spiritual essence present in each person through which
man can be completely illuminated. So, too, the Jewish
people has been chosen to teach and bring wisdom to all the
nations. So, when we sit in the *sukkah*, we should be glad
that we have been chosen for Hashem's shelter. At the same
time, we must exercise humility and not misuse our status.
We must serve as the soul and vitality for the world with our
teachings of justice and mercy.

---------------- ❖ ----------------

*T*he *mitzvah* of *sukkah* brings illumination and blessing
to the home. This light surrounds the home while the
illumination of the *mezuzah* protects the inner light from
harm.

---------------- ❖ ----------------

*A*nd they camped in Sukkos. (*Bamidbar* 33:5)

A king went out to look for a wife. After meeting many
women, he chose the one he felt would be most loyal. He
realized also that all the other women he had met would be
jealous. So he quickly took his chosen one, clothed her in
royal garments, took her to the palace and married her.
Now she was protected from the jealousy of the others. The
sukkah is the palace of Hashem. Here He surrounds us with
His protective tent and saves the Jewish nation, His bride,

from the jealous glares of the nations of the world.

———————— ❖ ————————

A nd they camped in Sukkos. (*Bamidbar* 33:5)
A wise king had many sons but one of them was outstanding in his commitment to his father. The king realized this and chose to groom him for a responsible position. When the other brothers heard this, they became very jealous and started to annoy the favored brother. To avoid this, the king called his favorite son and conferred with him in his private study. There, the king and his son were all alone; there, he was protected from the annoyance of the brothers. Thus, in the *sukkah* we too can experience a privileged privacy with Hashem.

———————— ❖ ————————

T he One who spreads a tabernacle of peace. (*Shabbos Tefillos*)
The Hebrew word for spreads is *haporeis*. The word *poreis* also means to break off a piece. The Jewish people are the chosen fragment of the world. They are responsible for teaching the path of Hashem.
But why is Hashem choosing a fragment rather than the whole? the nations ask.
The answer is that Hashem dwells within the brokenness. By breaking one's ego, one becomes a vessel for Hashem's dwelling. A vessel unbroken is not a vessel for Hashem. Therefore, the broken one is ready for absolute completeness and infinite wholeness while the unbroken one is really the incomplete one. *Haporeis*, when broken off, *sukkas*, can be a tabernacle, a protected area of peace, completeness and infinite calm.

The completeness of anything is in its vital part. However, the vital part is only part of the whole. Still, it is this vitality which lends value to the rest. We can compare this to food which is ingested by the body. There is vitality in the food although it is a small portion which makes the food worthwhile to eat.

This is the position of the Jewish people among the nations of the world. It is through the Jewish nation that the other nations come to share in Hashem and His teachings. When we sit in the *sukkah*, we realize our responsible to be the vitality for the world. We come before Hashem as broken vessels and are filled by Hashem's essence.

❖

*W*hen we prepare ourselves, we then have vessels for Hashem's goodness, illumination and light. There are, however, two sorts of light. One is inside which glows and fills us. The other is outside which surrounds us. One is our inner space, our mind and psyche, and one is our surrounding space, our life in the world. Likewise, our home too is filled with Hashem's light. The protection for the inner light of our home is the *mezuzah*. For the outside light, it is the *sukkah*. When we are in the *sukkah*, we are generating the protection of the divine light which surrounds our life outside of our home.

❖

*H*ashem's goodness is constantly flowing to the world. If there is a vessel to receive, then it becomes full. And how do we prepare ourselves to be the vessels for Hashem's goodness? We do this by opening our hearts to the fact of our creatureliness, our apparent lack of any substantial possession. We do this by verbally acknowledging that we are empty vessels before our Creator. This is prayer.

There are two types of prayer. One is a prayer when we are really and actually in need. We are empty, and our need is apparent. The other is a prayer when we are full and our need is not obvious. Each of these two conditions has an advantage and a disadvantage. When we are desperately in need, we naturally think of ourselves as broken vessels and need the help of Hashem's abundant goodness. But our thinking is not pure because we are desperate. What else can we do but beg? When we are full, however, our stance is pure. If we then stand before our Creator as a broken vessel, it is not out of need. Yet we still have a struggle. Can we acknowledge that all our fullness is from Hashem?

These are the two types of prayer cited in *Tehillim*. One is a prayer of the poor man. (*Tehillim* 102:1) The other is a prayer of Moshe. (*Tehillim* 90:1) To pray at a time when we are the poor man is certainly proper. After all, to whom should we address our problems if not to the Creator of the world. Yet it requires no great effort nor taking of a stance. The difficulty arises when we are not in need, because then our prayer is really a stance; it is a prayer of Moshe.

We can compare this to the child who was away from home and soon found himself penniless, lonely and desperate. He wrote a letter home telling his father how much he misses him and needs him, and he asked his father to please send some money. When the father received the letter, he realized that this was not a stance. His son had not yet realized how much he needed a father. The father knew that his son was in desperate need and that was why he had turned to him. Some months later, the boy was already employed and prosperous. Again he wrote to his father saying how much he misses him and that he needed him close by. The father then realized that his son had finally learned a truth about their relationship which he had not known until that time.

Sukkos is the time of our joy and gladness. It is the time of the year when we gather what we have sown, grown and reaped from the spiritual harvest of the entire year. We then pray a prayer of Moshe, the rich man's prayer. It is especially at this time that we must prepare our hearts as vessels for this goodness. We pray that what we receive should not go to waste but bring vitality to the whole of mankind.

❖

---

*I*t is written, Sound the *shofar* on the New Moon in the concealment of our holiday. (*Tehillim* 81:4) This refers to *Rosh Hashanah*, when the moon is still hidden. (*Rosh Hashanah* 86)

On the New Year all of mankind is judged. Then what is hidden? The Jewish people are hidden and concealed within the judgment of the world. Two weeks later, when the moon is full, the vital role that the Jewish nation has in the world becomes clear.

We can compare this to a teacher who is testing the class. During the test, the few who are devoted to their studies are hidden within the rest of the class. But as soon as the tests are marked, it becomes very clear whom this test has selected. When this revelation happens, the selected ones need protection from their jealous classmates.

This is the *sukkah*.

What was hidden on *Rosh Hashanah* is revealed during *Sukkos*. When we enter the shelter of the *sukkah*, the results of the judgments of *Rosh Hashanah* become clear to us and to all mankind.

32

*I*t is written, I remember the kindness of your youth, your love as a bride, how you followed Me in the desert, in the never-seeded land. (*Yirmiyahu* 2:2)

It is the virtue of the Jewish people. Since the Exodus, they are ready to discard all their worldly possessions and follow the path of Hashem. How is this?

The connection between Hashem and the Jewish people is not a coincidental one but one of essence. Their soul is essentially fused with Hashem. When an individual Jew subordinates himself to the Jewish nation, he can then taste this connection. He will then taste how important Hashem is to him.

We can compare this to the leaves on a tree. When a leaf acknowledges its essential nature as part of the tree, then it tastes a connection even to the roots. It is part of the whole tree. However, when one is arrogant and feels like an independent entity, he cuts himself off from his roots, which is Hashem Himself. One shows his arrogance by acting outside of Hashem's will, the Torah path. Then he becomes desensitized and incapable of experiencing his roots.

During *Yom Kippur*, we cleanse ourselves of our arrogance and redefine our being as an integral part of the people who walk the path of Hashem. We are then ready to part with our earthly belongings and walk with Hashem in the desert. This is the *sukkah*. When we move into the *sukkah*, we are uniting with our people. As we learned, all of Israel could suffice with one *sukkah* (*Sukkah* 27b); then we are ready to relinquish our possessions, our home and house, and be a part of the larger house, the house of Israel.

❖

---

*T*here is a divine order and providence, *hashgachah*

pratis, for each and every creature in the world. The amount each one of us is to receive and is receiving does not change. It is preordained.

Hashem's giving has two phases. The first phase is in the spiritual realm. The second phase is manifest in our physical life. In the first phase, the giving is infinite. When it reaches the second phase, it is already within a vessel and no longer possesses the quality of the infinite.

At least, so it seems!

The truth is that the limitations we experience are an illusion. Our habits and attitudes about the world are vessels and borders. Our body ends here; the object starts there. We experience the world physically in terms of borders and limitations; therefore, we conclude that it actually has limits. The experience of our bodies, however, is not the complete picture. Just beyond the illusion, the universe is without limit. The amount of providence we receive comes from Hashem. It has no limit. Yet, the infinite providence needs an infinite vessel, and we, who are of flesh and blood, are limited. How then do we receive infinite blessing from Hashem? It can happen only if we realize that our limitation, i.e., our ego, does not cause us to receive the blessing; it can only happen if we realize that all blessings come directly from Hashem. When one does that, one removes the concealment of appearances and encounters the true nature of the world.

It is written, Blessed is the man who trusts in Hashem, and Hashem will be trustworthy to him. (*Yirmiyahu* 17:7) To trust means to acknowledge that whatever you receive is because of Hashem's will and whatever it may be is good enough for you and could not be better. You trust His judgment in providing for you. Then what you receive is godly, infinite and limitless.

The opposite attitude is to think that what we receive is a

phenomenon unconnected to Hashem. This is idol worship. It is cut off from the roots and is dead matter. Idol
worship is a dead end; it is disconnected and dislocated
from the divine nature of the world. A person who takes a
stance of arrogance by disconnecting himself from Hashem
is a *rasha*, an evil doer. A *rasha* is considered dead; he has
broken away from the life and vitality in the universe. Thus,
when we enter the *sukkah*, we envelop ourselves in Hashem's
shelter. We trust in His protection and encounter the
infinity of Divine Providence.

❖

*T*he responsibility of the Jewish people is to reveal the
divine nature of the world, to remove the concealment and
demonstrate clearly and manifestly that Hashem is the
Master of the Universe.

One can do this work in three spheres: time, space and
spirit. Each of these needs restoration and uplifting. When
the various elements of a sphere are in proper order, then
the divine nature of that sphere is manifest. *Sukkos* is the
effort to bring the nature of space out of concealment and
demonstrate clearly that the world is full of His honor. The
walls and roof of the *sukkah* envelope holy space. We enter
a dimension of infinity which universal space represents.

Isn't this a contradiction? How can the infinity of space
become manifest within the apparent limitation of the
sukkah walls? This is precisely the beauty of the commandment. The path of Hashem, the *mitzvah*, breaks through the
limitation and encounters the infinite which is close at hand
and beyond the illusion. When we enter the *sukkah*, we can
free ourselves from all spatial limitations as we enter divine
space.

*T*he universe has divine order and unity; however, it is hidden from us by the material nature of the world. The apparent nature of the world is limitation, fragmentation and confusion. It gives us a false and mistaken impression; therefore, it leads us to untrue conclusions. The Jewish people are in the world to reveal Hashem's mastery and break through the concealment. Thus, they are in constant battle with the confusion of the illusory nature of the world. When they win, they restore and reveal its unity and divine essence.

During the battle, the Jewish people are designated by the name Yaakov meaning footstep; a battle is won by a systematic step by step approach. This approach is represented by Yaakov's ladder. When the battle is won, the Jews acquire the name Yisrael which means to do battle with divine forces and to succeed. This approach is by skipping and having a direct encounter with the true nature of the universe. Skip the steps on the ladder and affect the revelation of Hashem's presence in the world.

This is also represented by the *lulav* on the one hand and *sukkah* on the other hand. The *mitzvah* of *lulav* consists of four plants: the palm (*lulav*), myrtle (*haddas*), willow (*aravah*) and citron (*esrog*). Each one in turn represents a different level of mankind in the encounter with Hashem. Some are on a lower level and some are on a higher level. There are those with knowledge and deed (citron), those with only knowledge (palm), those with only deeds (myrtle) and those with neither knowledge nor deeds (the lowly willow). Levels are illusions manifest in the world of material things. The *lulav* is therefore Yaakov, the footstep going up the ladder one level at a time.

In the divine nature of the world, there are no levels at all. This is the *sukkah*; we skip to Hashem's shelter and meet Him directly as Yisrael. The battle is already won. There is no need for strategy and systematic warfare.

Therefore, *Yom Kippur*, a day of battle against concealment, falsehood and confusion, gives us the *mitzvah* of the
lulav, a gradual climbing step-by-step. Finally, we enter the
sukkah which is the truth of our condition; there really is no
confusion nor falsehood.

We can compare this to a king who took his loyal and
faithful servant and led him blindfolded into the dense
forest. He then sent soldiers to feign an attack, on the
servant. The servant battled valiantly. The soldiers convinc-
ingly played the role of a battling and retreating army. They
battled fiercely, but they finally withdrew. The servant had
vanquished the king's enemies! Now it is clear once more
that the king rules this forest, he thought. Suddenly, the
king came out of hiding. The servant soon realized that the
king had only been hiding, and the entire battle was nothing
but illusion. The king was present all of the time, and his
sovereignty was never in question. When we step into the
sukkah, we realize the divine nature of the world. We realize
that we are in a direct encounter with Hashem. We know
that although we battled, it was only to come to the ultimate
truth; no battle was necessary after all.

❖

---

*T*here are two opposing forces in the world. There is
Divine Presence and unity on the one hand, and there is
concealment and confusion on the other hand. The nation
which represents the former is the Jewish people; those who
represent the latter are the Amalekites.

With two opposing forces, when one is strong the other
weakens. As one becomes stronger approaching midpoint,
the opposition reaches its apex. Then the stronger begins
its decline and weakness.

When the Jewish people left Egypt, a revelation was about to take place which would have ended all concealment. This occurred when the opposition was strongest, and Amalek appeared for an attack. This was the appropriate time for the protection of the clouds which Hashem provided for them. Likewise, when we are victorious after *Yom Kippur*, the opposition is the strongest, and we need the protection of the *sukkah*. Thus, as we enter the *sukkah*, we remember that this time we are making a total commitment to reveal the Divine Presence in the universe. It is also the time that we are likely to experience the most opposition. We must take shelter within Hashem's protection, the *sukkah*, to withstand this opposition.

❖

*H*ashem is the master of the world; however, His dwelling place and presence is not manifest. It is concealed by the appearance and illusory nature of reality. It is through the work of the Jewish people that the concealment recedes and the revelation of Hashem's mastery is fully revealed.

This manifestation is called *Shechinah,* and it is the Divine Presence which pervades each part of the universe. In the *sukkah,* it is represented by inviting the seven patriarchs, Avraham, Yitzchak, Yaakov, Yosef, Moshe, Aaron and David, each one of whom was instrumental in the revelation of Hashem's presence in the world.

When there is concealment, there is also great yearning. Every particle in the universe yearns to be realized for what it really is and not according to appearances, illusions and the concealment of vessels. This is the meaning of the verse, In His shadow I have yearned to be . . . and I have stayed. (*Shir Hashirim* 2:3) Shadow is the period of concealment.

38

Moreover, there is yearning. This yearning is as strong as the degree of concealment.

During *Rosh Hashanah*, the concealment is very strong, as it is written, Sound the *shofar* during the New Moon in the concealment of our holiday. (*Tehillim* 81:4) The Jewish people are yearning for the revelation of Hashem's sovereignty, and they call out, "O King . . . reign over the world in glory!" This is the time of shadow and yearning. However, on *Sukkos* the *Shechinah* is revealed.

Our experience of *Sukkos* depends on our yearning for the *Shechinah*. As we enter the *sukkah*, we invite the patriarchs who strived for the ultimate revelation. We realize that we must participate to make Hashem's dwelling manifest; and if we do, we can rejoice with gladdened hearts.

———————— ❖ ————————

*T*he Jewish people have the responsibility to declare Hashem's kingdom. They must utilize their time and energy to realize that responsibility. There are many distractions to their attention; therefore, they must banish the distractions which work against their primary responsibility. They must focus their activities to fulfil their mission in the world. We accomplish this by separating from the other nations. We are then free from involvement which misdirects our energy. Our energy is then focused to accomplish our goal.

The Beis Hamikdash in Yerushalayim served this very purpose. It represented a private space for our people which made focused effort possible. The *sukkah*, too, is such a space. Therefore, during the holiday of *Sukkos*, sacrifices are offered for all the nations. When we are able to carry out our mission, then all the nations benefit. As the

Talmud says, If the nations would know how much they benefit from the Beis Hamikdash, they would decorate it with gold. (*Midrash Rabbah, Bamidbar* 1)

When we sit in the *sukkah*, we should realize how much benefit we could be to the world. We must prepare and consecrate our energies for this mission. Then the private space of the *sukkah* becomes charged with Divine Light that shines out in all directions.

3

CLOUDS OF GLORY

. . . that I caused the people of Israel to dwell in booths.

(Vayikra 23:43)

There is a disagreement among the sages. One says these were real booths. The other says they were clouds of glory which came in the merit of Aaron.

(Sukkah 11b)

The clouds came in the merit of Aaron, the *kohein gadol.* What did Aaron do which was of such special merit? He made peace between man and man. If two brothers quarreled, he went to one and said, "Your brother is very sorry for what he did, but he is too embarrassed to apologize. Please forgive him." Then he would go and tell the other one the very same thing. Thus, Aaron prevented the fabric of the Jewish nation from coming apart. Similarly, the clouds of glory protected them from all harm, as a tent of fabric protects those inside.

Aaron brought peace in two types of quarrels. One was between people who quarreled because of a misunderstanding. Aaron helped them see their mistakes and regain their friendship. The other type of quarrel was between people who had actually wronged each other. These people, too, Aaron reconciled. He embraced them and showered them with love. In turn, they were very embarrassed and repented with all their hearts and souls.

The clouds, too, in Aaron's merit protected those who were worthy and those who really were not worthy. Likewise, a *sukkah* protects all. It stands as a protection of love over all Israel, and it urges those who are far to be far no longer.

❖

*I*n booths you shall dwell for seven days. (*Vayikra* 23:42) The Torah is instructing us: Go out of your permanent dwelling and go live in a temporary one.

The world functions according to natural laws. We become comfortable with the routines of nature that we witness every day. If the sun rose today, it is sure to rise tomorrow. We feel its reassuring constancy; it is our permanent dwelling. It is that aspect of the universe which we experience as a constant. On the other hand, there is also the unexpected, dynamic and miraculous. This is the divine aspect of the world with which we have contact from time-to-time; it is its temporary aspect. We can hardly expect to relate constantly to the miraculous aspect of the world. After all, our senses tell us constantly that this world is what it appears to be, nothing more and nothing less.

The Torah, therefore, commands us, Go out from your permanent dwelling, and from regarding the world as permanent. It tells us to move into the temporary and experience the divine and the miraculous, as it is written, So that your generations should know that I caused the people of Israel to dwell in booths when I took them out of the land of Egypt. (*Vayikra* 23:43)

How will you know from sitting in your *sukkah* what Hashem did many generations ago?

The answer is, because we were liberated from the ordinary laws of nature at the Exodus; therefore, we can again experience that liberation. Hashem promised the Jewish people that they will never fall into the enslavement of the world of nature again. They were given wings with which to rise above the ordinary world and go to the *sukkah*, the dwelling of the Divine. As it is written, And I will lift you on the wings of eagles and bring you to Me. (*Shemos* 19:4)

———————— ❖ ————————

*A*fter the cleansing of *Rosh Hashanah* and *Yom Kippur*, we are ready to be on the level of the miraculous and the divine.

The *Midrash* tells the following parable. When a farmer reaps his crop, the stalks argue with the kernels. The stalks say, "It is because of us that all the planting was done!" The argument continues until the farmer threshes his crop. The straw and chaff are allowed to be blown by the wind while the kernels are gathered together and stored. (*Midrash Rabbah, Bereishis* 39)

The same way Avraham stood among the peoples of the world. The peoples thought that they would have the responsibility to declare Hashem's kingdom. Then Hashem spoke to Avraham and said, "Go forth from your land . . . to the land that I will show you." (*Bereishis* 12:11) It then became clear who had been chosen for that awesome responsibility.

Another parable given by the *Midrash* is that of a beach-comber who was sifting sand on the beach hoping to find treasure. As the sand fell through the sieve, he kept saying, "No, this is not what I was looking for." But soon the sand emptied from the sieve and a diamond appeared. He called out, "Yes, this is it! This is why I let all that sand fall through the sieve, just to find this diamond!" (*Midrash Rabbah, Bereishis* 39)

Likewise, the nations of the world were together with the Jewish nation in Egypt. The nations thought, Surely ours is the responsibility of Hashem's work in the world. As soon as the Exodus took place, the Jewish nation followed Hashem into the desert. It then became clear which was the grain and which was the chaff.

Similarly, every being in the world is judged on *Rosh Hashanah* and *Yom Kippur*. There is suspense; everyone is judged equally. Then the judgment is over. The Jewish people go into their *sukkah*, the tent of faith. Suddenly, it is clear who is innocent and who is guilty. Therefore, *Sukkos* is called *Chag Haassif*, the Holiday of Ingathering. Just as the harvest of wheat from the field makes clear which is the grain and which is the chaff, so too does the *sukkah*.

The *sukkah*, therefore, is firmly linked with Avraham and Aaron as we read, I remember the kindness of your youth, the love of your gatherings, when you followed Me in the desert. (*Yirmiyahu* 2:2) "The kindness of your youth" refers to Avraham who initiated the youth of the Jewish nation. "The love of your gatherings" refers to Aaron whose energy came from the congregation of the Jewish people. Avraham took himself aside to one side of the river and set up his tent.

Aaron distinguished himself by working for the unity of all the people.

When we sit in the *sukkah*, we know that all the judgments, pains and hardships we endured were to establish our innocence and our willingness to walk with Hashem even "in the desert."

———————— ❖ ————————

*A*nd they journeyed from Ramses and came to Sukkos. (*Shemos* 12:37)

The Jews only reached Sukkos in the special merit of Aaron. How so?

Hashem sent Moshe to perform a complete redemption; however, the Jewish people were suffering so greatly that they had no patience to listen to Moshe. Therefore, Moshe took along Aaron who was a pillar of kindness; this kindness gave the people the strength to be redeemed. As it is written, . . . that I made them live in *sukkos* . . . when I brought them forth from Egypt. The *sukkah* is supported by the pillar of kindness. Thus, whoever wants the blessing of kindness should connect himself to the *mitzvah* of *sukkah*.

———————— ❖ ————————

*H*ashem is the ultimate perfection. When this perfection manifests itself in our own flesh-and-blood life, then we can say that Hashem's kingdom is being revealed. This is the *Shechinah*: unity and peace.

There is another aspect of Hashem's being which forever remains concealed. This is the essence of Hashem which is unknown and inconceivable. The latter is the fact that Hashem is King, the former is His kingdom. Hashem as King is Heaven; Hashem's kingdom is earth.

The two brothers, Moshe and Aaron, related to these two aspects of Hashem. Moshe related to Hashem the King, and Aaron to Hashem's kingdom. Moshe ascended to Mount Sinai and carried down teachings for the people of Israel. He linked the Jewish nation with the unknowable and hidden, and he brought the Word of Heaven to the earth. On the other hand, Aaron unified the Jewish nation by making peace. He made Hashem's kingdom manifest on the earth.

In essence, what was Aaron's work? He brought together people who were separated from each other, from the Jewish nation and from Hashem. He made them realize that at the root level everyone is connected to the other, that all divisiveness is an illusion. It is only on the level of husks, the very outside of things, that there is any division. At the root, there is only unity.

Thus, Aaron's work was to make manifest the everpresent connection and unity of all and to make clear the all-encompassing nature of Hashem. Therefore, everything is subordinated to His protection. These were the clouds of protection in the merit of Aaron. This is also the tent of protection, the house of Hashem, the *sukkah*. Its purpose is to bring everything in the world under Hashem's wings and shadow.

When rust accumulates on us, we have difficulty seeing the connectedness of our roots. Consequently, after *Rosh Hashanah* and *Yom Kippur*, when we remove the dross and rust, it becomes clear that we were never actually separated. We immediately enter into the *sukkah*. There, we again experience our unity and oneness with each other and with Hashem.

———————————— ❖ ————————————

*M*oshe and Aaron each related to a different aspect of Hashem. The life of our teacher Moshe was one of struggle. When he was born, he was cast into the water. He struggled at Pharaoh's palace and in the work fields among his brethren. He struggled to flee Egypt, and he had no rest at the well where he met his future wife. He struggled with Pharaoh until Pharaoh released the Jewish people; but neither did Pharaoh nor the Jewish nation give him any rest. He struggled with the angels to receive the Torah; then again he struggled with his own people when they made the Golden Calf. He struggled with the Amalekites, as it is written, When Moshe lifted his hand, the Israelites were victorious; when he lowered his hand, the Amalekites were victorious. (*Shemos* 17:11) The path of Moshe was *netzach*, victory, and this required struggling. The disadvantage of this path was and still is that one cannot always be victorious. There can be situations when a battle is lost.

The path of Aaron was different. His approach was to create situations where battle and struggle are not even necessary. Therefore, Aaron is the peacemaker, and he makes offerings in the holy tabernacle, the *Mishkan*, which expiate the sins of the people. He prevents plagues and pestilence from attacking the entire community. He even removes accidental murders from among the Jewish nation, and he minimizes evil thoughts from their minds. His way is *hod*, honor, and the one who emulates him does not struggle for honor. One receives honor by virtue of one's deeds.

In the Kabbalistic scheme of divine attributes, *sefiros*, these two paths of victory, *netzach*, and honor, *hod*, reach a balance in foundation, *yesod*. The active and passive paths of victory and honor of Moshe and Aaron are the foundation of the Jewish nation. Therefore, the clouds of glory are in the merit of Aaron. There is no struggle, but there is the de facto peace and honor. Likewise, it is the honor which one gains when one sits in the *sukkah*.

❖

Sukkah is the foundation of peace.

It is written, "Peace, peace to the one who is far and to one who is near," says Hashem. (*Yeshayahu* 57:19)

One who is near is the *tzaddik*, the righteous one who has never sinned. While this world is incomplete and full of strife, the *tzaddik* can still reach some measure of completeness and peace.

One who is far is the *baal teshuvah* who is returning to Hashem after going astray. He brings completion and peace from the highest place, for he is considered even higher than the *tzaddik*.

The *tzaddik* is represented by Moshe who dwelled in the mountain with Hashem for forty days. The *baal teshuvah* is represented by Aaron who was involved in the making of the Golden Calf. Therefore, *Sukkos*, which comes after the days of repentance, is in the merit of Aaron. When we have turned again to Hashem as our refuge and sit in the *sukkah*, we receive peace from the highest place.

The kindness of Hashem spreads without limit and pervades the minutest particle of the universe. It is this kindness which is the essence of each and every item in existence. The kindness of Hashem is infinite and indestructible. The vessels, the husk, the illusory appearance of things are only limitations, and they ultimately must perish.

The permanence of things is Hashem's lovingkindness in them. The stronger we are connected with this love, which ignores the apparent separateness of the husk, the more we are vessels to receive the unity and oneness which characterizes the *sukkah*. The *sukkah*, the protection in and by the lovingkindness of Hashem, unifies all souls in divine infinity.

The activity which thickens the finiteness of the creaturely world is sin. Therefore, it is also that which produces a gap between creature and creature, and between creature and Creator. Thus, after *Rosh Hashanah* and *Yom Kippur*, when the cleansing is complete and purity returns to the soul, it is open again to the infinite love of Hashem. Then one can walk directly into the *sukkah*, the dwelling of divine infinity.

Separation is only an illusion. By treading the path of the Torah, we lessen the illusion, and the true nature of the world becomes apparent. Returning to Hashem is the act of connecting to the essence and ignoring the illusory aspects of existence. After *Yom Kippur*, we are pure and have thinned out the illusions of our separateness. We are more in touch with the truth about this world, and we sit in the shelter of Hashem, the protection of the *sukkah*.

4

THE KINDNESS OF YOUTH

The word of Hashem came to me, saying, "Go, and proclaim in the hearing of Jerusalem, 'Thus says Hashem, I remember the kindness of your youth, your love as a bride, how you followed Me in the desert, in the never-seeded land.' "

(Yirmiyahu 2:2)

H ashem's lovingkindness fills the world. Liberation and illumination flow from Him constantly. However, this kindness needs to enter the world of flesh and blood. It enters this world when we do good deeds rewarded by Hashem's kindness. We become worthy of His generosity because our physical deeds bring the kindness into the material world.

There are times, however, when the infinite kindness of Hashem miraculously enters our lives without vessels. Such kindness has no place in this world and is lost. What can we do to keep this miraculous kindness? We must quickly flesh it with deeds. Then it can remain with us forever.

This was precisely our predicament when we left Egypt. We were liberated miraculously and without being deserving. Therefore, we needed to bridge the infinite kindness to this world through our deeds. As the prophet says, I remember the kindness of your youth . . . when you followed Me in the desert. This infinite kindness became permanent in the form of clouds of glory which surrounded the Jewish nation. Flesh-and-blood deeds bring the kindness of Hashem into physical vessels which protect it from disappearing.

When kindness has vessels, it can even stand up to the scrutiny of judgment. It is protected. Therefore, after *Rosh Hashanah* and *Yom Kippur*, days of judgment, it is clear that we deserve Hashem's kindness. We have prepared vessels for it through our good deeds, and it has the protection of the *sukkah*.

I "remember" the kindness of your youth . . . After an event happens, it no longer in the world. It is finished, yet it can be remembered. Memory is a vessel for events which otherwise would no longer be in the world. Hashem's kindness during the Exodus would have ceased to be if we would not have made vessels for it. Therefore, it can be remembered, for "memory" is its vessel and protects it from utter extinction.

The *sukkah*, too, is the materialization of our good deeds and a remembering of Hashem's kindness. The strength of our *sukkah* experience is directly related to how much we deserve Hashem's lovingkindness. May we all be worthy of it.

———————— ❖ — ·· ————————

*I*n each and every object in the universe, there is a speck of divine vitality, its essence and soul. If this essence would be manifest, there would be no doubt that Hashem is the master of the world. But it is concealed, and so is Hashem's sovereignty. It is concealed in the material world of illusion and masks of falsehood. Nevertheless, it is in man's power to reveal the divine roots and essence of the world. He can do this by godly deeds. By acting according to the Torah teachings, he uncovers the divine nature of the world. Then the concealment is but a garment for Hashem's presence, and the Holy Name of Hashem then rests upon the individual.

When the whole Jewish nation helps reveal Hashem's kingdom, He is called the Lord of Israel. The Jews are then but a garment for Hashem's presence, and they are powerfully tied to His essence and vitality. This connection protects them and is their tent of peace. (In Hebrew, the word for tent, *ohel*, has the same letters as *Eloha*, the Lord.)

Peace is the manifestation of Hashem's kingdom in the world. War comes from divisiveness, contradictions and opposition, quarrels and differences. These qualities are born from the material sphere of illusion. The true essence of the world is in its unity in Hashem. Hashem is one, and He brings peace.

The *sukkah*, too, is the garment which the Jewish people wear after their hard labor throughout *Rosh Hashanah* and *Yom Kippur*. They worked strenuously to reveal Hashem's Name in the world. They have connected strongly to the divine roots and now have peace. When we sit in the *sukkah*, we all realize how rooted we are in the Master of the World; we are one and, thereby, we have peace.

❖

And they journeyed from Ramses and camped in Sukkos. (*Bamidbar* 33:5)

In Ramses they were slaves. Their only master was Pharaoh, a being of flesh and blood; their only credo was limitation. However, in Sukkos the opposite was true. Their master was now Hashem, the creator of Heaven and earth; their credo was liberation.

But how is it possible to change so quickly from a slave mentality to a constant divine consciousness of free choice? In natural circumstances it is hardly possible. But it was a miracle. The infinite or divine aspect of the universe came into contact with the nation of Israel. This encounter made it possible for them to make the transformation. Nevertheless, miraculous events are only temporary. We can no longer come to the liberated place of Sukkos without a great deal of hard work. Therefore, each year, *Sukkos* is preceded by *Rosh Hashanah* and *Yom Kippur*, the days of awe which are the preparation to move out of bondage and the worship of the material world to freedom and worship of our Creator. Thus, the energy of *Sukkos* remains in our flesh-and-blood life.

In booths you shall dwell for seven days . . . (*Vayikra* 23:42) The gateway of the infinite world is open to man. He enters the divine order of the universe, and all limitations vanish. Thus, this liberation from slavery brings great joy and renewal.

When an individual is a slave, he slowly loses his will. Each free area of his life is slowly enslaved by the master. Soon there is no area in which he exercises desire or will. However, in the *sukkah*, which is the house of Hashem and the gate to freedom, there is a renewal of desire and yearning. The heart and mind are alive again and full of joy.

❖

*T*here is an inner order and an outer order. The latter is the world of appearance and material reality. This is the world we encounter with our senses; it is the world of illusion.

A more complete picture of the world is that Hashem's honor fills the universe. (*Yeshayahu* 6:3) Its true nature is divine and infinite. Our experience with it, however, is finite and limited. Why? Because the world presents itself as finite, and we react accordingly.

In order to encounter the infinite which is the world, we must prepare ourselves. We must be proper vessels to relate to it. If we are not prepared, we are likely to miss such contact even if we happen to find it by chance.

We can compare this to a newborn baby. The baby has fingers, but they are yet too weak to grasp anything but the lightest objects. If he should happen to grasp something a bit heavy, he'll very likely lose it. He lacks the vessels to contain it.

When the Jewish people left Egypt, they had not yet formed the proper vessel to encounter Hashem. Yet they did encounter Him when they crossed the Red Sea. During the crossing of the Red Sea, even a maid saw more than the prophet Yechezkel. (*Mechilta, Beshalach* 2) They had no firm grasp on this encounter, and they almost lost it.

Why is it so easy to lose spiritual gains? Because there is a spiritual balancing in the world. When illumination and enlightenment increase, so do the energies of concealment, confusion and ignorance. There is an internal dynamic in the universe. On the one hand, life; on the other, death. On the one hand, growth; on the other, desolation—a desert.

This is symbolized by the Jewish nation leaving Egypt and journeying through the desert. The desert is not only empty of growth; it is full of harmful animals, such as snakes and scorpions. When the vessels are being formed, one needs protection. Therefore, Hashem hid the newly-born nation inside the protective clouds. These would protect them from both the spiritual as well as the physical opposition.

When the vessels are being formed, there is a struggle. One must expend great energy to retain the encounter with the Divine. To contain within them the revelations of the Exodus and the Red Sea, the newly-formed nation had a most difficult struggle. Moreover, on the physical level, they had to struggle with the Amalekites.

When a person struggles, his energy is not focused on his ultimate goal. He wastes energy just to retain his position. If the struggle is won, then he can again refocus all his energy toward that final goal. Thus, before the Jews are in the *sukkah*, they are struggling. This is the great effort of *Rosh Hashanah* and *Yom Kippur*. Finally, when the struggle is over, they can walk directly to an encounter with Hashem. This is the *sukkah*.

If one is willing to move away from comforts and smugness, go to the desert, seek Hashem, prepare vessels, then one can enter the house of Hashem, the *sukkah*, and receive His protection. Therefore, when Hashem will judge the world, at *Mashiach's* coming, the *sukkah* will be used. And this will be the sin of the nations, that they will refuse to celebrate the holiday of *Sukkos*. (*Zechariah* 14:10) The nations will not leave their smugness and risk an encounter with Hashem.

When we leave our houses to walk into the *sukkah*, let us be prepared to risk. To struggle until our vessels are developed enough to receive the divine nature of the universe and to live in the protection of Hashem's house.

❖

*I*t is written, So that your generations should know

THE SFAS EMES ANTHOLOGY

that I caused the people of Israel to dwell in booths when
I took them out of the land of Egypt. (*Vayikra* 23:43) There
are two opinions concerning the word *sukkos*, booths. One
says the *sukkos* were clouds of glory, and one says they were
actual booths. (*Sukkah* 11b)

The clouds which protected the Jewish people in the
desert were a clear indication of Hashem's presence. This
was so because it was clear to the generation of the Exodus
that Hashem was among them. When it is clear to us with
unbending faith, then it is also reflected in the material
world. When our faith weakens and we are confused by the
illusions of our senses, the Divine Presence also slips into
obscurity and concealment. The protective clouds disap-
pear, and only the frail, little *sukkah* is left. Still, Hashem's
spirit is everpresent with us, and it is not removed one iota.
Only the appearances have changed.

We can compare this to a prince who started out on a
journey. The king sent faithful guards to protect him from
all harm. The guards travelled at his side. One day the
prince had an argument with the guards. The guards
became enraged and refused to travel at the prince's side.
They did not dare disobey the king's wishes, so they hid in
the forest and continued along with the prince. They
protected the prince until he reached his destination. The
prince was sad when the guards left him. Still, when he
noticed his horse and saddle with the king's seal, he
remembered his father's promise to bring him home safely.
He was consoled. He did not know how his father was doing
it, but he trusted that his father's protection was constantly
with him.

So, too, when we enter the *sukkah*, the tent of faith, we
remember the promise of our Father in Heaven to protect
us always. He is always with us with His Divine Presence and
the clouds of glory. Furthermore, when we look at the walls

with pure faith, we know that they are not the temporary walls of illusion; we see them as permanent walls from the world of truth. They are not the finite walls of material but the infinite ones of spirit.

❖

*W*hen Hashem created the universe it was full of light with which one could see from one end of the world to the other. (*Midrash Rabbah, Bereishis* 5:1) The true nature of the world is divine, and it has a quality of unity. The vessels, however, are material, fragmented and opaque. We see only that which is in front of us: borders, limitations and superficiality. Our senses encounter the vessels, and that is as far as we see.

We must recognize the impermanence of the material world. Then the supernal light will be able to shine through its opaqueness, for we will be in touch with the divine nature of the universe. Our attitude toward the world as temporary brings us closer to the permanent. Therefore, the degree with which we connect ourselves to the impermanence and frailty of our physical *sukkah* will be the revelation of the Heavenly *sukkah* of clouds. The more we are aware of the illusory nature of the world, the stronger will be our connection to the permanent and divine nature of the world.

This also happened to Avraham. Because he left the illusory world of his father's idol worship, he was told by Hashem to go "to the land I will show you." (*Bereishis* 12:11) When we turn our backs on ignorance, we are able to see the promised land. Our eyes become vessels for the Divine Light which shines from one corner of the universe to the other. We are told by the Kabbalists that the word *sukkah* means to see. As we turn our backs on the illusion of permanence, which our homes represent, and run to the *sukkah*, our eyes open. We can then see our life and that of the universe from one end to the other.

—————————— ❖ ——————————

*W*hen Hashem liberated the Jewish people from Egypt, He wished to elevate them spiritually. He devised a path for them that is above the natural world in order that they should be connected to the miraculous and divine aspect of the universe. As it is written, And Hashem did not lead them through the land of Pelishtim. (*Shemos* 13:17) The words *derech eretz*, meaning through the land, also allude to the way of the land, the natural, material and illusory world.

The *Zohar* relates that had they been worthy the Jewish people would still have the Beis Hamikdash. They sinned, therefore, they lost that level of holiness. But, through repentance, we can return to that abandoned path. After *Yom Kippur*, the day we return to Hashem with all our hearts, we are given a glimpse of the Beis Hamikdash. Though we seem to be "here" within our physical boundaries and limitations, we are actually "there" in the Beis Hamikdash. Those who have returned to Hashem become vessels to taste the miraculous world. This is the *sukkah*.

When *Mashiach* will come, Hashem will remove the protective covering which shields us from the sun, and He will ask everyone to come into the *sukkah*. Those who have become accustomed to the comfort of the material world will not be able to tolerate the brilliant, spiritual light. Only those who yearn for a high level of spirituality will be prepared to receive that unique illumination. Thus, in the *sukkah* it becomes clear that our return has been a complete one. We can then bask in the sunshine of Divine Light and revelation.

*T*he Jewish people are vessels to receive the Divine Light and to relate to the miraculous aspect of the world. In Egypt, they were enslaved and saturated with the illusory, transitory and superficial nature of the world. In Egypt, their universe became dense and opaque, limited, fragmented and ordinary. Then Hashem shone His light onto them, and they tasted the sweetness of the infinite world. They gathered their few belongings and set out to follow the Master of the Universe into the desert.

As divine vessels, the Jewish people did not find their place in Egypt. Their place in the world was only with Hashem, with the miraculous. Therefore, after the Jews left Egypt, they went to Sukkos, which was Hashem's place. Likewise, each year after *Yom Kippur*, we cleanse ourselves from the opaqueness of our relationship with this world. Then we go directly to the *sukkah*, Hashem's place, our place. There we find our home and our true nature.

———————— ❖ ————————

*T*he *sukkah* reminds us of the clouds of protection that surrounded the Jewish people. What was their merit? The Jewish people ran to Hashem for their refuge. They put themselves completely in Hashem's hands, and Hashem received them completely.

Why were they able to do this? Because the slavery of Egypt was unbearably painful. Upon the first opportunity, they ran to Hashem's shelter lest they fall back into the clutches of their oppressors.

This happens also on a spiritual level. We all are capable of choosing, and Hashem grants us the freedom. There are times, however, when our choices are so mistaken and painful that we would rather not have any choice. All we want is not to tread on the mistaken path. Then we ask

Hashem, "Lead us in a straight path." (*Tehillim* 27:11) You lead us, Hashem. We don't want to choose!

We can compare this to a man who was overweight and could not adhere to his diet. Finally, he developed complications and had a severe heart attack. The doctors were barely able to save his life. They warned him that if he continued to eat excessively, he would die. He hovered between life and death for a number of weeks.

Finally, he was out of danger, and he spoke to his doctor. "Please do something so that I will never again have this condition. I don't ever want to feel this kind of pain and fear of death again."

He chose not to have a choice rather than to face the consequences of a poor decision.

During *Rosh Hashanah* and *Yom Kippur*, we realize that our behavior is leading us to ignorance and death. We turn our hearts from the mistaken paths and proceed towards Hashem's shelter. This is done out of fear of pain which awaits us if we remain in our present condition. When *Rosh Hashanah* and *Yom Kippur* have passed, we sense the purity of our hearts. We realize the great lovingkindness which Hashem has granted us. He has taken us under His protection, changed our hearts and drawn us near to Him. We forget about our pain and fear, and we run to His shelter with great love. This is the *sukkah*.

We can compare this to a father and a child who strolled together among the rosebushes. After a time, the child was not careful and walked into the thorns. The child cried bitterly while his father scolded him to be more careful. A little while later, the child again stumbled into the thorn bushes and burst into tears. This time he held up his hands to his father to lift and carry him lest he stumble and hurt himself again.

His father reached down and lifted his child. The boy

snuggled into the warm embrace of his father. He felt the safety and comfort of his father's closeness. Suddenly, he forgot about the thorns lurking below among the rose bushes. His only thought was about how much his father loved him and how wonderful that felt.

When we are in the *sukkah*, we realize how secure it is to be in Hashem's shelter. Our minds are filled with the love Hashem has for us; our fear of our painful mistakes recedes in to the background. We are home.

5

FOLLOWING YOM KIPPUR

*And Hashem said to Moshe: On the tenth day of
this seventh month is the Day of Atonement; it shall
be for you a time of holy convocation, and you shall
afflict yourselves and present a fire offering to
Hashem. And you shall do no work on this day, for
it is a day of atonement, to make atonement for you
before Hashem your Lord. For whoever is not
afflicted on this day shall be cut off from his people.
And whoever does any work on this day, that person
I will destroy from among his people. You shall do
no work, it is a statute forever throughout your
generations in all your dwellings. It shall be to you
a sabbath of solemn rest, and you shall afflict
yourselves on the ninth day of the month beginning
at evening, from evening to evening shall you keep
your sabbath. And Hashem said to Moshe, Say to the
people of Israel, On the fifteenth day of this seventh*

*month and for seven days is the Feast of Booths to
Hashem.*

(Vayikra 23:26-35)

H ashem promised . . . not one will be cast away. (*Shmuel*
14:14) Not one Jewish soul will be cast away from
returning to Hashem. Rather, each one will have the
opportunity to cast off his evil ways and to return to the
shelter of Hashem. Not only does Hashem allow you to
return, but He opens His hand wide and helps in every way.
Open up for me in your hearts a tiny opening, the size of a
needle's eye, and I will widen it as the gates of a palace.
(*Midrash, Shir Hashirim* 5:3)

We are glad that Hashem allows us to return, yet it does
not seem just to extend such help and kindness to sinners.
"Where is justice?" the evildoers ask.

The answer is that justice decrees that everyone receives
what he deserves. There are many who have purity, holiness
and goodness, yet are unable to make it real because of
overpowering circumstances. Hashem in His great mercy
smooths the difficulties, and the purity, holiness and goodness are transformed into reality. Then justice says, "This
person truly deserved kindness. Look how beautifully he
did."

We can compare this to a king who had summoned his
subjects to the palace for a great feast. It was a three day
journey to the palace. On the second day, there was a severe
rainstorm. The waters loosened huge stones from the
mountainside and uprooted trees. The floodwaters formed
the stones, trees and mud into a thick wall which blocked
the path to the palace. When the king's servants reached the
wall, they became confused and discouraged. The wall was
impregnable; it hardly seemed possible to cross over it.

Many of them turned back dejected and went home. But others refused to surrender. They began to pull bits and pieces from the wall with their bare hands. Hearing of their loyalty, the king quickly sent soldiers with equipment and dismantled the wall. The servants arrived at the palace and thanked the king for his kindness. Their hearts were filled with joy and gladness as they sat down for the great feast.

When the others who had turned back heard of this, they complained. "Why did you help them come to the palace?" they grumbled. "They didn't deserve it more than we! It isn't just!"

The king answered, "When I took away the obstacles, I didn't do it for them! I only wanted to see who was really on the way to the palace, and who was really on his way home!"

Those who arrived at the palace were on their way to the palace.

The *sukkah* is the dwelling place of Hashem, for it is written, And I will dwell with the humble . . . (*Yeshayahu* 57:15) Those who humbled themselves during the days of atonement were treated with justice. Hashem removed the obstacles, and it became clear where they were heading.

───────── ❖ ─────────

*A*ny haughty spirit is an abomination to the Lord. (*Mishlei* 16:5)

Since Hashem is the supreme Master, every other creature is merely one of His dependents. By their arrogance they are denying His presence. This impossible mission of driving out Hashem's presence from His own world must instead deprive these arrogant people of their true place in this world.

But when these arrogant people return to Hashem, they give up their false claims and thereby regain a true place in this world. Moreover, Hashem returns to them more than they deserve because of His bounteous kindness.

The *sukkah* is an infinite space for the arrogant ones who have humbled themselves on *Yom Kippur*. The *sukkah* is the palace of Hashem, and we enter it with great humility so that it can be entirely filled with Hashem's Divine Presence.

❖

*T*he Holy Blessed One wanted to create the world with strict justice but saw that the world could not endure. He therefore combined it with lovingkindness. (*Midrash Rabbah, Bereishis* 31:1)

To receive all our needs in strict justice, we would need to be perfect. Perfection in this world of Hashem's creation is inconceivable. For each created thing is in need of its creator and is intrinsically lacking and imperfect. Only with lovingkindness and mercy can our world survive.

At times, we become self-righteous and start to believe we are entitled to our existence and all its benefits. When this happens we are triggering a dangerous reaction. By pleading innocence and righteousness, we cut off our claim for clemency, and we could cause Hashem's compassion to be held back. But when we acknowledge our limitations and our shortcomings we are once again candidates for Hashem's many mercies. That recognition restores to us at least a small claim for Hashem's blessings.

On *Yom Kippur*, we all stand before Hashem with real humility, time and time again we implore Him to grant us mercy and not judge us according to the letter of the law. Now we can enter the *sukkah* with a feeling that we are justly entitled to entry in to Hashem's palace.

❖

When the world was created, Hashem said, "Let there be light," and there was light. (*Bereishis* 1:3) And so for every creation, Hashem said, "Let there be . . ." and there was. These pronouncements took the will of Hashem and transformed it into material reality. But the word of Hashem not only created the world, it also causes the world's continued existence, as it is written, With the word of Hashem the Heaven was made; and with the breath of His mouth, all its hosts. (*Tehillim* 33:6)

The words of Hashem, however, are hidden within the material world. They are concealed to the senses. Only through faith in the Almighty, who constantly breathes life into His world, do His words become manifest. Conversely, our faith finds its expression in words—the words of prayer. Then our words reach inward and uncover Hashem's word within the material world.

When we use words to emphasize our human role in the world we are distancing ourselves from the word of Hashem. This arrogance negates faith and empties our prayers of meaning. When we humble ourselves, we can again relate to the primeval words of creation and recite our faith.

The fast and prayer of *Yom Kippur* restores our humility. We pray all day long, bringing an increasing contact with the word of Hashem.

At a deeper level, the word of Hashem is within each of us. Did not Hashem say, "Let us make man in our image"? (*Bereishis* 1:26) This word is concealed within the human body and sense experiences. Suffering and pain humble us and the word of Hashem within us shines forth. The word within comes in contact with the word of Hashem everywhere in creation, and suddenly we are praying. At that moment we are redeemed from the spiritual exile of Hashem's concealment.

Now we are ready for the *sukkah*. The *sukkah* is a space

containing the word of Hashem, and we are enveloped within it. We have arrived.

———————————— ❖ ————————————

Sukkos is described in the Torah as *Chag Haassif*—a harvest festival. Harvesting wheat requires us to remove the unwanted portion—the chaff. Then the grain is separated, the best part is taken as food, the rest for animal feed.

A similar selection process takes place on *Rosh Hashanah* and *Yom Kippur*, as we are told: Three books are opened on *Rosh Hashanah*. The purely righteous are written and sealed for a good life. The purely evil ones are written and sealed for death. Those in between are pending till *Yom Kippur*, if they repent they receive life. (*Rosh Hashanah* 16b)

After the separation of the chaff, the grain is taken home. We enter the *sukkah* with resolve and purity. It is a clear sign of where we stand with our commitment to Hashem.

———————————— ❖ ————————————

*T*he Jewish people left Egypt and shortly afterward stood at Mount Sinai. There they received the supreme revelation and teaching of all time. Forty days later, when Moshe did not return to them at the expected time, some of the people demanded an idol to guide them. Aaron reluctantly suggested to them that they might collect gold jewelry. When they presented him with the gold, he flung it into a fire and out of the fire emerged a golden calf. Aaron later felt terrible remorse for his role as an accessory to idolatry, although he had hoped to stall for time until Moshe returned, and he repented.

Later, Aaron was chosen to work in the Holy Tabernacle, the Mishkan, and he was the only person allowed to enter the Holy of Holies, the *Kodesh Kadashim*, once a year.

What made Aaron worthy to have such a close encounter with Hashem?

A servant of the king once rebelled. His disobedience took place before the entire royal court, and the king angrily banished him into exile. Some time later, the servant humbled himself and realized his great error. He was too embarrassed to go directly into the palace, so one night he hid in back of the palace and tapped on the window of the throne room. The king turned and saw his former servant. He opened the window and listened to him beg forgiveness and express a complete humbling before the royal presence. The king told him to dig a secret passage near the back wall leading into the king's private chamber. This was done, and the former rebel met intimately with the king.

The king said, "You can't come in through the front gates because of the opposition. I must therefore take you in through a different path, but then we can even be alone and have a closer encounter."

The righteous walk through the front door of the palace and have an encounter with Hashem. The penitent ones, *baalei teshuvah*, must dig their way into the palace in secret and unused paths. This path leads to the Holy of Holies, an intimate encounter with Hashem. This was Aaron's entrance into the Holy of Holies on *Yom Kippur*. Even if Moshe was on the highest level, still it was Aaron who came through the secret passageway and was able to come into that most holiest of places.

Yom Kippur is the collective repentance and return of the Jewish people, immediately afterwards we are ready to come into Hashem's palace and have an intimate encounter with Him. This immediate encounter is the *sukkah*. The *sukkah* may be rustic and modest in appearance. It may look like the back of the palace, but it is precisely where one can be close to Hashem.

Let us enter with humility and joy in order to be worthy of such closeness.

———————— ❖ ————————

*H*ashem is the Master of the world. Yet He chooses to conceal His mastery within the creation. The natural world of cause and effect appears as a world without a master. That is why we call it a world of untruth and illusion.

When the truth is manifest, so is the kingdom of Hashem. Then it becomes clear that the world is His creation and He is the root of all power. Each and every item of Creation, from the highest to the very lowest, is dependent on Hashem. The total revelation of Hashem's control of creation would be the sight of the entire throne of His glory. But the awareness of this sublime truth is almost a vision of the throne of Hashem on this earth.

At the same time, the Throne of Honor represents also a rarefied spiritual perception of the Creator. This ultimate spiritual awareness can rarely be reached. Yet one who returns, a *baal teshuvah*, reaches the Throne of Honor. (*Yoma* 17b) Why is this so?

Every sin is an expression of doubt as to whether Hashem really cares about the actions of a mere mortal. When the sinner recognizes the need to repent, he is aware that even a lowly creature like himself is ruled by Hashem. This conviction is like seeing the *Kiseh Hakavod*–the throne of Hashem's glory. It also raises the *baal teshuvah* to the *Kiseh Hakavod*. The *baal teshuvah* ironically becomes the link to Hashem's presence, a link from the Highest to the lowest; therefore, the *baal teshuvah* is catapulted from the lowest point to the highest.

On *Yom Kippur* we have all tried to achieve the status of the *baal teshuvah*, we have all acknowledged with our professions of guilt that Hashem is all powerful and that there is none beyond His grasp. We have all come close to that particular link to the *Kiseh Hakavod*. Thus, after the repentance of *Yom Kippur*, the Name of Hashem becomes manifest. The *sukkah* is the worldly representation of Hashem's throne which we have reached by repentance. When we, as *baalei teshuvah*, enter the *sukkah*, we proclaim Hashem's kingdom from the highest to the lowest.

———————— ❖ ————————

*A*s an apple tree among the trees of the forest, so is my beloved . . . to sit in its shadow was my yearning and I did stay. (*Shir Hashirim* 2:3) The apple tree has very little shade and people avoid sitting under it. But the Jewish people persisted and sat under its shade. (*Midrash, Shir Hashirim* 2:3)

The kingdom of Hashem which brings tranquility and peace is concealed in this world. One must have faith to believe it is there and be consoled by its strength.

It is comparable to a king in exile who was still served by some of his faithful servants. Others mocked the servants for following a king who no longer had any power. The servants answered, "Perhaps it seems to you that the king is powerless. But wait! You will see that he still rules this land!" Some time later, the king returned to his capital with a powerful army, recaptured the palace, ruled the land once more and rewarded his loyal servants.

When Hashem's kingdom is concealed, his relationship with the Jewish people is also concealed. On *Rosh Hashanah*, when judgment is meted out to every human being, the Jewish people are concealed. They are concealed within the judgment of the whole world, and it is called . . . in the concealment . . . (*Tehillim* 81:4) After *Yom Kippur*, however, the righteousness of the Jewish people becomes clear, and they are vindicated. The King, too, returns to His palace. Again, it is manifest that He is the ruler, and one can find protection in His shade. This is the shade of the *sukkah*.

When we sit in the *sukkah*, we become aware of our unique good fortune to see the shade of the *sukkah*.

❖

*M*an cannot live without Hashem even for an instant. When he realizes this, a great yearning awakens in his heart. He yearns to have a meaningful encounter with Hashem and to possess illumination, wisdom and holiness. He realizes that without this he is but a broken vessel, empty and constantly in need of fulfillment.

On the other hand there is some satisfaction in the fulfillment of material needs, and this dulls the spiritual yearning. Enjoying one's own self-sufficiency can be an obstacle in yearning for Hashem, and awareness of deficiency arouses greater craving for His proximity.

Therefore, on *Yom Kippur* when we negate our physical needs, we are humbled before our Creator. When we feel the emptiness of our lives, we yearn for the fullness of a life with Hashem. This yearning prepares Hashem's blessings and goodness.

Our deficiency is in three dimensions: space, time and life. The yearning for a spiritual space is the holy land of Israel; spiritual time is the World-to-Come; and spiritual life is the Torah, the path of life.

These three dimensions are represented by the *sukkah*. The *sukkah* is a holy space. The festival of *Sukkos* is a time for peace (*Koheles* 3:8), a foretaste of the World-to-Come, and a vessel for life—since we enter it after being granted life on *Yom Kippur*.

When our yearning is awakened on *Yom Kippur* by the pain of denial, we are ready to enter the *sukkah*. In the *sukkah* we arrive at the fulfillment of our deepest needs and desires.

---- ❖ ----

On *Sukkos* in the time of the Beis Hamikdash, thirteen bullocks were offered up the first day, twelve on the second day, and so on until on the seventh day seven were offered up, amounting to seventy in the course of the whole festival. These seventy bullocks correspond to the seventy nations of the world.

The essence of each creature is rooted in divine existence. When our deeds reflect this, then Hashem's presence is manifest and Hashem's kingdom is at hand. The concealment of His presence is *galus*—exile. The divine and holy sparks which reside in every particle of creation are then inactive. There is an emptiness, a gap and yearning for fulfillment. Deeds which reveal the holy sparks prepare the one who performs them to receive Hashem's kingdom.

The era in which Hashem's kingdom will be totally revealed is called *Olam Haba*, the World-to-Come. Those who have prepared in this world will be allowed to experience the World-to-Come.

Still, not only the righteous do good deeds. What happens to the good deeds of evildoers? This energy is transferred to the righteous. Their commitment to the revelation of Hashem's kingdom empowers them to redeem those holy sparks. As it is written, And I have separated you from the nations . . . (*Vayikra* 20:36) This means that Hashem has separated you to reveal His Name; however, from where does your energy come? . . . from the nations . . . You receive the energy from the occasional good deeds of the nations. This is the reason for the offerings during *Sukkos* for all the nations of the world. The turning point of *Yom Kippur* puts us in a position to gather the holy sparks from the nations.

Rosh Hashanah removed the wraps from the kingdom of Hashem. In our prayers then we constantly declaimed, "*Hamelech*–The King!" This is followed by *Yom Kippur* when we prepare to be recipients of His kingdom.

The *Zohar* tells us that a *baal teshuvah* restores all his tattered garments, and they become vessels for divine revelation. Therefore, the *sukkah* is a vessel restored, for it is created from the sins of the penitent.

It is written, Praised is he whose sins have been uplifted and whose transgressions are covered. (*Tehillim* 32:1) Covered means by a garment. A garment was made out of his transgressions. Likewise, the roof covering of a *sukkah* must be made of the undesirable portion of the grapevine and grain. This teaches us that our *sukkah* is created from our undesirable actions, the sins and transgressions for which we have repented on *Yom Kippur*.

When we sit in the *sukkah*, we can become connected to its highly charged energies. Our sins were brought about by arrogance, evil yearning, jealousy, stubbornness, rebellion, anger, cynicism, lying and cheating. Now that we have returned to Hashem, all those energies and strong emotions are transformed and channeled into the holiness of the *sukkah*, the service of Hashem, and into the revelation of His Kingdom.

❖

*Y*ou should rejoice in your holiday, and you should be only joyous. (*Devarim* 16:14)

What is the opposite of joy? When we are in need, there is no joy. When our yearnings are unfulfilled, our desires unsatisfied, then too we have no joy. Joy comes when our present-self and who we want to be are united.

We are creatures created by the Master of the Universe. We have no real power other than that given us by the Master. The desire for independent power is a form of rebellion against Hashem, and the more we become involved in the pursuit of independent power the more we forfeit our status as creatures of Hashem. On the other hand, when we are comfortable with our limitations and our dependance on Hashem, we are restored to our natural goodness, and that restoration brings joy.

There are varying degrees of comfort with dependence. On the simplest level, we realize our physical limitations and frailties and know that our bodies are prone to illness and breakdown, that life hangs on a delicate thread. We know that despite our great accomplishments, we are but a small step away from death and oblivion. We are grateful to the Master of the World for keeping us alive and sustaining us in our everyday struggles.

On a higher level, we can acknowledge more of the greatness and awesomeness of Hashem's existence. We realize that the vast expanses of space and the tiniest particles are all filled with Hashem's glory. We accept that He has made, is making and will make everything that there ever was or will be. Then the soul is filled with awe, and the mind starts to acknowledge total insignificance. We shrink from illusions of grandeur to our true size before Hashem's mighty power.

On *Rosh Hashanah* and *Yom Kippur*, the Days of Awe, we realize our insignificance as we stand in judgment before Hashem. When we realize that we have at least become wise enough to recognize this reality, we joyfully enter the *sukkah*, and we rejoice with our Creator, the Master of the World.

❖

*Y*aakov gathered himself and his children, and this saved him from the intrigues of his brother Esav. (*Midrash Rabbah, Bereishis* 32:8) Similarly, the *sukkah* is a shelter from the intrigues of our accusers of *Rosh Hashanah* and *Yom Kippur*. (*Midrash Rabbah, Bereishis* 84:1) Therefore, it is called the holiday of gathering. (*Shemos* 34:22) Even the *lulav*, the tallest of the four species around which the others are gathered, is symbolic of Yosef, the righteous one. In Yosef's dream he saw, And behold we were gathering sheaves in the field, and mine stood up and all of you gathered around . . . (*Bereishis* 37:7) So too is the *tzaddik*, the righteous one, who leads those around him in the proper direction toward Hashem's shelter.

❖

*H*e spreads over us a *sukkah* of peace. (*Shabbos Tefillos*) The *sukkah* is Hashem's shelter. It brings us back to fulfillment, harmony and peace, all of which are found in Hashem. Hashem is the source of all the good which exists in the world. He also placed in each us of us a drop from that holy fountain. Though only a drop, it has infinite potential. This drop of holiness is always in the human soul, always sacred and always pure. But when a person sins, the drop of holiness loses some of its power to influence the entire person.

A transgression blocks the life-giving waters from our spiritual wellsprings. At first the outer edges of our being dry up and wither. But if we continue on the path of falsehood we block the waters at their roots and totally wither away.

Then Hashem sees our sorrowful state and helps us experience an encounter with Him. The intensity of this encounter breaks through all barriers and clears all the debris in the path of the spring of life. We have returned to Hashem and to His shelter. This occurs in the days of *Rosh Hashanah* and *Yom Kippur*. As it is written, Peace to those far away, and to those that are near. (*Yeshayahu* 57:19) Peace is experienced when the soul revitalizes our physical being.

But arrogance does not allow Hashem's encounter to be felt, and so arrogant people remain cut off from that drop of holiness. As it is written, And the evildoers are as the tumultuous sea . . . (*Yeshayahu* 57:20) They cannot experience tranquility and peace.

Because we are reconnected to our roots and source of life we can go directly into the *sukkah* of peace. When we sit in the *sukkah*, our hearts are open to the spring of life which bubbles forth from us. We can revitalize every cell in our body, every utterance of our speech and every concept and image of our thoughts. In the *sukkah*, we can experience harmony and peace coming from the infinite roots of our Creator.

---- ❖ ----

When I sit in darkness, Hashem is a light for me. (*Michah* 7:8) Fortunate is the nation that knows the sound of the trumpet, Hashem, they go with the light of Your Countenance. (*Tehillim* 89:16)

How do we experience light and darkness? We experience light when our eyes respond to a source emitting light energy. When no energy is being emitted, or if our eyes cannot receive the light, we experience darkness. Our eyes receive certain wavelengths of light energy. They are not proper receptors for ultra-violet and infra-red light. However, we can assist our eyes by using instruments which are sensitive to those extremes of light. Even if no other light is available and it is apparently dark, the instrument sees everything; and there is light.

Hashem fills the universe with light, but we can only receive a limited amount of this light. For the portion of light for which we have no receptors, it might as well be dark. We simply have no way of experiencing it. It is dark for us, but in truth the light is at its greatest intensity. Even when I sit in darkness, I still know that Hashem is a light for me. His intense light must be there, but I am not worthy of experiencing it.

The lovingkindness of *Sukkos* is hidden in the Days of Awe of *Rosh Hashanah* and *Yom Kippur*. Thus, it is written, From distress I have called Hashem, and He answered me in a large place. (*Tehillim* 118:3) Although the Days of Awe seem full of judgment and tightness, when *Sukkos* arrives, we see the expanse that was concealed in them. Likewise, Peace to those far away, and to those that are near. (*Yeshayahu* 57:19) At first it seems that Hashem is far away, but then one realizes that it is actually because of His closeness.

When we enter the *sukkah*, we experience the lovingkindness of Hashem which is too intense for our receptors. We gain strength for the whole year when the darkness seems so real to us. We then know that the intense light of Hashem is there all the time.

❖

*T*he Holy Blessed One wanted to create the world with strict judgment, but He saw that it would not survive. He,

77

therefore, blended it with lovingkindness. (*Midrash Rabbah, Bereishis* 1)

Whenever something is being created, kindness is blended in to the world again. This happens when one turns to Hashem in repentance and becomes as a totally new creation: there is a new flood of kindness.

Avraham crossed the river to be on the side of Hashem while the others stayed behind with their idol worship. He then circumcised himself. This was a promise that not only he but also his children would stay with Hashem, for it is written, And he sat by the door of the tent . . . (*Bereishis* 18:1) It means that, by turning entirely to Hashem, Avraham opened up the door of kindness which became his seal and lifework.

When Aaron returned to Hashem after the incident with the Golden Calf, he received the virtue of lovingkindness in great measure. He was now connected to that door, and he could open it for others. Thus, he became an angel of love and peace among his people. When we turn to Hashem after *Yom Kippur*, we are ready to enter the door of the tent, the *sukkah*, a new house built with the virtue of lovingkindness. The world is created once more, and each one has a new chance to obtain life.

❖

*I*n descending order, there are three spheres of creation: creating, forming and doing. Corresponding to this is the soul, spirit and life of man which vitalizes him. When man sins, he disrupts the order in the celestial and spiritual spheres. When man wants to restore the three spheres, he returns to Hashem. He first returns in the sphere of doing which are his actions; he straightens them to correspond with holiness. Then he corrects the sphere of forming which is his speech. Finally, he needs to restore the sphere of creation. This sphere has the closest connection to the Creator, and it is the most difficult to reach. It can only be obtained by divine mercy, for it is written, Return to me, and I will return to you. (*Zechariah* 1:3) Therefore, when a person returns to Hashem with all his heart, then he is created anew. Moreover, the individual, who has just been created, is still connected to the energy of the Creator and is fitting to be in His shelter.

Hashem's shelter is the *sukkah*. When we enter, we go as newly created beings who still taste the energy of the creative moment. We are able to open our eyes anew in order to see the glory of Hashem and to praise His Name.

❖

*H*ashem has made man upright, yet they sought out many calculations. (*Koheles* 7:29)

When a person follows the Torah, he is directed towards Hashem and has singularity of purpose. Otherwise, he has a multiplicity of desires and flounders in aimlessness. These are the many calculations of the one who is astray and disconnected from Torah holiness. When we return to Hashem on *Yom Kippur*, we again affirm our singularity of purpose and are made straight again. We know exactly where we are going, and we go directly to Hashem's shelter.

❖

*T*he repentance which is valued most is born out of joy, not out of fear. During the Days of Awe, *Rosh Hashanah* and *Yom Kippur*, we are very conscious that our lives and our future hang in the balance. We cannot help feeling that we must repent to avoid the bitter fate of the *rasha*. Although this repentance is born of fear rather than of joy, Hashem, nevertheless, accepts it and us.

As *Sukkos* follows the *Yamim Noraim*, the Days of Awe, we have only just emerged from the court of judgment. Which thinking person did not feel small and inadequate on those awesome days, as he answered for his deeds to his Creator?

That sense of being small and inadequate reminds us that we are not entitled to our portion in this world. Now we feel the loss of space, the loss of entitlement to space in this world and that we are guests in this earth at Hashem's pleasure. By giving up our claim to space in this world, we can enter Hashem's space—the *sukkah*.

The *sukkah* is Hashem's space which He gladly shares with those human beings who can bring themselves to take up no space—those who became humbled on the *Yamim Noraim*.

With this goal of demanding no space for ourselves in mind, we can understand why the *sukkah* has space for guests, and potentially for an unlimited number of people. As the Talmud says, Why is the word *sukkos* written in the Torah without a *vav* (the singular form *sukkas* would be written that way)? Could the entire Jewish people sit in one *sukkah*? To teach you that a borrowed *sukkah* is sufficient for the *mitzvah*. (*Sukkah* 27b) Since the *sukkah's* occupants feel that they need no space there is the necessary hypothetical possibility of the entire Jewish people sitting in one *sukkah*.

The more we feel humble in the *sukkah* the more we preserve it as the domain of Hashem, which we rightfully enter as a reward for our own sense of unworthiness.

6

A Shelter of Faith

*Come and see, when a man sits in this dwelling,
a tent of faith, the Divine Presence, the Shechinah,
spreads her wings over him from above, and Avraham
and the other five righteous ones come to dwell with
him.*

(Zohar)

*Whoever has a share in the holy nation sits in the
tent of faith and greets the guests, to be full of joy in
this world and the World-to-Come.*

(Zohar)

I n the shadow of wisdom is the shadow of silver. (*Koheles*
7:12) The *sukkah* is known in mystical writings as the
shadow of wisdom. It is also the shadow of silver, for the
root letters of silver indicate that it represents desire, and

the *sukkah* is the shadow of man's desire for proximity to Hashem.

There is a very high level of conduct governed by the head's wisdom, and a low level governed by instinct, symbolized by the feet. (The Hebrew word *haregel*—the foot, is from the same root as *hergel*—habit.) One can be led by wisdom or by instinct. The feet need to be constantly enlightened by wisdom.

There are two corresponding realms of the spirit. One is a spiritual abode created from Hashem's infinite wisdom. The other is the fruit of human desire to be closer to Hashem. That second abode seeks to encompass not only deliberate rational acts of man, but also the simpler instinctive deeds. For the rational, wise aspect of human life seeks to acquire control of the instincts, too. Everyone should have the ambition to share spirituality with the total person not just the higher mind.

A person's feet follow the head, apparently as an act of faith. The *sukkah* is an emanation of Hashem's wisdom. But it is a place for admission of the entire person, mind and instinct, spiritual being and creature of habit together. That is why it has a second name in the *Zohar, tzila d'meheimenusa,* the shadow of faith, those who have faith are admitted regardless of whether they have attained wisdom.

---------------- ❖ ----------------

*M*any waters cannot quench love . . . (*Shir Hashirim* 8:7)

The love between Hashem and the Jewish people is unquenchable and is constantly present. When they sin, the love is concealed. The universal repentance of the Days of Awe causes it to be revealed once more.

The *sukkah* is that revelation of Hashem's love for the

Jewish people. It is a shelter, a place where each heart can find a home and protection. Even those who have sinned and returned are now included, for it is written, Love covers all sins. (*Mishlei* 10:12)

------------------- ❖ -------------------

A nd Hashem said, "Let there be light," and there was light. (*Bereishis* 1:3) What happened to this original light? It was hidden for the righteous in time to come. (*Midrash Rabbah, Bereishis* 1:3)

When Hashem formed and created man, the human being was barely above the other animals. His distinction was in his being created in Hashem's image. This does not refer to the physical form of man, but to the sharing of some of the attributes of Hashem. The awareness of Hashem is a level of perception that animals cannot share. The ability to create language, thought and concept is a divine attribute graciously shared with humans. The ability to create speech is the vital point of differentiation between the animal and the human, as the Torah says, And Man became a living being. (*Bereishis* 2:7) The *Targum* interprets this to mean a speaking being.

Man is the crossover point between Hashem's existence which is infinite, and the world He created which is finite. We touch both spheres. We are creatures of material and finite needs, and we are creators with infinite potential at the same time. We see with the same optical vision of the animal, yet we can use this sight to recognize Hashem in the world and proclaim His Name.

Which light shines infinitely from one end of the world to the other? The Name of Hashem, because it is the revelation of the infinite, must transcend all physical limits. When can man see with this light? The answer is when he relates totally to being the image of Hashem. Therefore, the light had to be concealed when man was not worthy.

When Avraham came and proclaimed the Name of Hashem, the creation was renewed. It is written, And He called them man when they were created. (*Bereishis* 5:2) Our sages say, Read it not *behiborom*—created—but as *b'Avraham*——with Avraham. The world was created anew with Avraham, because Avraham willingly assumed the role intended for man in creation—to create and recreate the universe. He, therefore, saw with the supernatural light from one end of the world to the other. He called in the Name of Hashem—he showed people how Hashem's glory is revealed in each and every item of the creation.

When we proclaim the Name of Hashem, we separate ourselves, as did Avraham. He crossed the river in order to separate from the idol worshippers and to proclaim Hashem's glory.

The *sukkah* is the resting place of Hashem's Name; it is a microcosm of the world. Although it is limited in space and time, it embodies the infinite quality of both. When we enter the *sukkah* we assume the original role of man as the link between the material world and the infinity of its Creator. We are restored to all the blessings Hashem destined for mankind at the time of creation, and therefore, the *sukkah* is the root of all blessings for the year round.

———————————— ❖ ————————————

*H*ashem watches over us constantly without interruption, yet He conceals His interest. Only in times of unusual closeness is this attention totally revealed. It was revealed during the wanderings of the Jewish nation in the desert from Egypt to the Promised Land.

The *sukkah* brings us back to that era of special and total protection. We enter it with complete faith as our forefathers did in journeying through the desert. We leave our home and walk into a temporary dwelling to stay with Hashem in complete faith and trust. Thus, we are surrounded by the clouds of glory in a shelter of Hashem; and this reminder of His constant watchfulness is with us at all times.

❖

*W*hat defines a free man and a slave? A free man has the power to decide the course of his actions. A slave not only owns nothing but is also controlled by his master. Therefore a commitment from a slave is worthless since he will not have the option of fulfilling it. The slave does not own his own body, even his capacity to produce children is the possession of his master. The physical form of the slave is totally cut off from his decision-making power, which is the essence of self.

Thus we see that the hallmark of freedom is the link of the human body to the decision-making ability.

We are all dependent on the infinite power of Hashem. If we cut ourselves off from the source, our limitations become manifest; and we wither and die. When we are servants of Hashem, we are free. When we cut ourselves off from Him, we becomes slaves.

Those who do not recognize their total dependance on Hashem are soon cut off from their divine roots and are slaves. When the Jewish people attempt to break away from Hashem, they become slaves unto slaves. They become enslaved to the arrogant nations of the world. They then realize that they have exchanged true freedom for miserable slavery.

Aaron constantly worked to unite the Jewish people with

Hashem. Because he was successful, the Jewish nation was free from foreign domination. In this special merit of Aaron, the clouds of glory surrounded and protected the Jews in the desert.

7

A TEMPORARY DWELLING

In booths you shall dwell for seven days.

(Vayikra 23:42)

The Torah has stated, leave your permanent dwelling place and dwell in the temporary dwelling.

(Sukkah 2a)

The rabbis taught: All the seven days one makes the sukkah the permanent dwelling place and his home as if temporary. How? If he has beautiful vessels, he brings them to the sukkah and beautiful spreads, too; he eats, drinks and lounges in the sukkah.

The rabbis have stated: You shall dwell . . . (Vayikra 23:42), as you dwell all year in your home.

(Sukkah 28a)

And I will give you paths among these stationary beings. (Zechariah 3:7) The angels are referred to as stationary beings. They experience Hashem on such a high level that they stand immobile before Hashem. They are awed by His infinite majesty and stand absolutely still.

While on a journey, one must keep moving; but when one arrives, one is still. There is nowhere else to go.

Man, however, is different. He must constantly move, climb to higher levels and accomplish his mission on earth. He climbs from level to level, consolidates his position, then moves upward again. He gains experience, synthesizes that experience with his essence and advances again. The way of man is to move, stand and proceed until the end of his days.

When man has found Hashem on whatever level, he is then standing still. It is a very safe and secure position. But how will the kingdom of Hashem become known? Until the Name of Hashem is accepted and known throughout the creation, man may not rest. It is dangerous to venture from the safety of the position already obtained, but we have no choice.

Avraham had grown and developed his knowledge and fear of his creator, now he had found safety and a spiritual home. But Hashem said to him, "Go out from your country, your birthplace and your father's house to the land which I will show you." (*Bereishis* 12:11) This was the instruction given to Avraham and all his descendants to go forth and proclaim Hashem's kingdom to the world.

Where do we obtain the great faith needed for this leap in the dark?

When we stand in absolute awe before our Creator and recognize and become totally aware that we have neither power nor existence without Him, then we can step forward bravely and rise confidently to new levels of serving

Hashem. When we have acknowledged that we are, as we say in the *Yom Kippur* prayer, "A shadow of a bird passing over the field, a withering flower, crumbling clay . . .," then we can climb further. We experienced this awareness during the Days of Awe of *Rosh Hashanah* and *Yom Kippur*.

On *Yom Kippur*, our souls are at their peak of yearning, and we are elevated to the level of angels. The angels sing, "Praised is the Name of the honor of His kingdom forever and ever." (*Yoma* 35b) Whoever recites the song means to say, "We are not independent; all we can say is that Hashem's kingdom is for ever and ever." Therefore, we too recite this prayer on *Yom Kippur*. Like the angels, we also stand in awe of the great mercy and kindness showered on us by our Creator on *Yom Kippur*. Again, we stand very still.

At the end of the Days of Awe, our sins have been forgiven; we are as a newborn child. Our spiritual strength has been renewed. We are strong in our faith and yearn to follow the path of Hashem. We are now ready to journey forth. Go forth from your country . . . Get out of your permanent dwelling and go into the temporary one. (*Sukkah* 2a) We go forth to proclaim Hashem's Name in the world, for it is written, And you shall love Hashem with all your heart, all your soul, all possessions. (*Devarim* 6:5) You should make Hashem beloved . . . (*Yoma* 86a) This is the essence of the *sukkah*—our love for Hashem and Hashem's love for us.

Walking out of the house on the way to the *sukkah*, we take a step with complete faith. There are no doubts in our minds; there is only the absolute and complete trust in Hashem. For no matter where we go, He is with us in all His strength and glory.

———————— ❖ ————————

*F*or I am your passing guest, a sojourner, like all my fathers. (*Tehillim* 39:13)

The soul of man is strong enough to last for all eternity. But the body eventually reaches a time limit and is gone. Nevertheless, the body, whose existence is most fragile, seems most real. The material world is destined to disintegrate. It is the only world we can know, but it eventually turns into a form which is unfamiliar and unrecognizable.

The bodies of humans and animals are destined to return to the earth and become transformed into another part of existence. A time will come when nothing of their current existence will be identifiable in this later form. The reality of the world is more of an illusion than a reality.

The soul, however, is both eternal and infinite. It is the combination of both of these factors, the physical and the spiritual, which is the total person. When we are in touch with our total being, we realize that we are passing guests on the earth. Therefore, Avraham was told, Go forth from your country . . . (*Bereishis* 12:11) It is a lesson he immediately had to learn. This earth is not as it appears. We are here but for a short time, and we must soon move from our place. The place we occupy is temporary, and we must soon relinquish it. Go forth . . . is the truth about our very being.

Sometimes, we get lost in this world of illusion. The temporary and unsatisfactory nature of this illusory world leaves us dissatisfied and miserable. For the eternal soul longs for the permanent spiritual world, and we seek and journey to Hashem. Go forth . . . is our connection to our forefathers who totally understood the need to flee from the world of illusion and find Hashem's permanence.

We leave our illusory permanent house and go into the *sukkah*. Go forth . . . we can hear Hashem's command, and we follow enthusiastically.

*T*here is a discussion in the Talmud regarding whether a *sukkah* should be a temporary building or a permanent one. (*Sukkah* 21b) Conceptually, both these opinions are correct, for the *sukkah* which appears temporary, represents the permanent nature of the world.

We are leaving a home and entering our *sukkah*, pitching a tent to proclaim the eternity of Hashem's Name. It is, therefore, the most permanent dwelling anyone can have, for it assures the revelation of Hashem's kingdom on this earth.

❖

*T*he Talmud concludes that the *sukkah* need not be a permanent dwelling. (*Sukkah* 21b) The *sukkah* is the shadow of Hashem. There we encounter Hashem on the level of the World-to-Come. Such an encounter with Hashem is not for the masses but for the *tzaddikim*, the righteous, who walk constantly with Hashem. Everyone else is yearning and striving to be with Hashem, yet does not attain it. This yearning, however, is valued by Hashem as much as the entire World-to-Come.

Therefore, the *sukkah*, which can hold all the Jewish people, is temporary. Let us leave our permanent way of being with Hashem. Then we can yearn for a level of total closeness, the World-to-Come. Although we cannot maintain this way permanently, at least we can experience it temporarily.

8

THE FOUR SPECIES

And you shall take for yourselves on the first day the fruit of a beautiful tree, branches of palm trees, and boughs of leafy trees and willows of the brook, and you shall rejoice before Hashem your Lord seven days.

(Vayikra 23:40)

A nd you shall take for yourselves on the first day the fruit of a beautiful tree . . . (*Vayikra* 23:40)

Sukkos is the time when Hashem draws nearer to the Jewish people with great love, and we draw closer to Him. We experience the abundant shower of blessing and love that comes to us from Heaven, and we are inspired to move toward Hashem.

Sukkos is the last of the holidays of the year. Each one adds a dimension to the ultimate knowledge, the knowledge of Hashem. *Sukkos* brings this to completion and sustains it for the entire year. Therefore, it is written, So that your generations should know that I caused the people of Israel to dwell in booths. (*Vayikra* 23:43) *Sukkos* is the holiday of knowing, and it is a blessing bestowed on us by Hashem. We prepare to receive Hashem's blessing in the depths of our heart. It is also written, Take unto yourselves . . . (*Vayikra* 23:40) Take the blessings until you are full.

The *Midrash* compares this to a king who invited some of his servants to his private dining room. They never before had this privilege and were reluctant to eat. The king said, "Would I invite you if I did not want you to eat?" Similarly, Hashem is saying to us, "Take! When I am giving in abundance . . . take unto yourselves . . ."

The beautiful fruit is the *esrog*, a citron. Its shape indicates that it symbolizes the heart. It reminds us to fill our hearts with the knowledge of Hashem and to retain this for the entire year.

Since we have purified our hearts on *Yom Kippur* and prepared them for Hashem's blessing, we are ready on *Sukkos* to be united with the entirety of Israel; it is this union which makes our purified hearts better vessels to receive Hashem's blessing.

This is symbolized by the four types of plant species. The humblest of them is the willow, it has neither taste nor smell. This symbolizes those Jews who have neither good deeds nor Torah. Even they, if they join together with the rest of the nation, will receive Hashem's blessings.

———————— ❖ ————————

*T*here are two aspects of the world. One is the reality of our senses. This is the material or real world. The other is the divine aspect of the world, which we have no vessels to perceive.

The Torah teaches us a path, a way of life, which is true to the actual nature of the world. Hashem's kingdom, honor and glory, are contained within the illusion of material reality, but they are sparks of holiness trapped in the mundane world. *Mitzvos*, Torah deeds, reveal the divine aspect of the world and release the sparks of holiness.

Some *mitzvos* raise the holy sparks of the inner nature of things. Others reveal divinity even in ordinary physical nature.

To understand how this happens visualize a critically ill patient whose doctors had already given up hope of a recovery. Finally, a great specialist was found at the far end of the earth, and he agreed to treat the patient. His method was to have the patient regain his interest in life, health and strength. The healer spoke softly but firmly; his encouraging words sunk deeply into the patient's heart. Slowly, the patient moved from his despair and became encouraged. His resolve improved, and he wanted to live; however, there was no improvement in his condition. When asked about the patient's condition, the healer said, "It will take some time until you will see an improvement in his body. But once the mind is working properly, the body is sure to follow."

Sukkah is a *mitzvah* which affects our inner consciousness, for it is written, So that your generations should know that I caused the people of Israel to dwell in booths . . . (*Vayikra* 23:43) The *mitzvah* of *sukkah* restores a pure knowledge deep in our hearts. Yet, *Sukkos* is a time when all of Israel gathers together in joy and happiness during the harvest time. This gathering was a national assembly in the time of the Beis Hamikdash. When all of Israel is together, they have an energy and power to break through all obstacles and barriers.

Therefore, we gather in the *sukkah* and tie the four kinds

of plants together. Every part of our body, every type of Jew from the lowest to the highest, restores the outside material world while Hashem's wisdom sinks inside into the deepest part of us.

———————— ❖ ————————

*T*he *sukkah* is Hashem's shelter and garden. It is the Garden of Eden and the World-to-Come. Nevertheless, the Jewish people would not be satisfied with that, for they want some part of this holiness in their own hands. Therefore Hashem gave us the *mitzvah* of the four plant species.

After *Yom Kippur*, the Jewish people emerge humble, pure and holy. They feel the enmity of the arrogant, and they run to Hashem's shelter, the *sukkah*. They are safe there and happy, yet they want more. They desire to hold onto the shelter itself and rejoice with Hashem, their Creator. This is fulfilled with the four plant species we hold so lovingly in our hands.

———————— ❖ ————————

*S*pirituality is enhanced by wisdom and good deeds—Torah and *mitzvos*. Similarly, plants are enhanced by both flavor and fragrance. The *esrog* has both, and it symbolizes those who have both Torah and good deeds. Some people only have wisdom, and this is the *lulav*; while others only have good deeds, which is the *haddas*. Still others have neither, and this is the willow, *aravah*.

The great yearning to be close to Hashem can only be evoked if we all join together. Our yearning is beyond reason, and so is our chosenness. Hashem chooses even those who are not worthy. Therefore, in order to gain entry into Hashem's shelter, we must humble ourselves totally and join even those whom we consider the lowliest of our nation. In truth, they are held in the same regard as the most worthy among us.

Therefore, we need not take the *arba minim* on *Shabbos*, because it is a day when all of Israel comes together anyway. The secret of *Shabbos* is, says the *Zohar*, that all gather together in the secret of the one. All souls find their place together with all the others, and there is unity and peace.

———————— ❖ ————————

*T*he four kinds of plants represent the parts of the body. The myrtle branch or *haddas* symbolizes the eyes; the willow leaves or *aravah* the mouth; the citron or *esrog* the heart; the date palm leaves or *lulav* the spine. When we hold these four, we consecrate the energy of our entire body to Hashem. This is no easy feat to accomplish. But the power of this great *mitzvah* helps us achieve this goal.

Each *mitzvah* is a promise that the deed is possible. When Hashem commands, "Honor your father and mother," or when He commands, "You shall not steal," it is a divine promise that these *mitzvos* will be in the realm of the possible. Circumstances may present obstacles, but we will have the capacity to perform them. Thus, the four plants of the *mitzvah* of *lulav* are a promise that one can focus the entire body energy toward Hashem, no matter what powerful forces act against it in this world.

———————— ❖ ————————

*S*ukkos is a time of joy, as it is written, You shall rejoice in your holiday. (*Devarim* 16:14) True joy is when the soul is in its natural place, well-rooted there and nurtured by the source of life. This is accomplished with humility and a

96

feeling of being the most modest among all of Israel, for the soul of the entire nation is attached at its core to divine holiness. Each individual is fed from this fountain of life and wisdom, for it is written, And you should take for yourselves . . . (*Vayikra* 23:40) Each one should take the holiness which suits his own soul.

The Jewish people humble themselves and do not even take what is offered. They go to Hashem Himself even if they have no vessels for it. As it is written, The King had brought me to his private chambers, I will be glad and rejoice with You. (*Shir Hashirim* 1:4) Although the king has offered me the innermost chambers, the deepest levels of spirituality, still I will be happy only with Him. When we hold the *lulav, esrog, haddas* and *aravah* together, we join all of Israel to seek only Hashem. May it be our will always.

❖

*W*hat is prayer? When we pray, we manifest faith and yearning. When we have neither wisdom nor good deeds— we pray and yearn for Hashem's help. Since there is prayer in the world, evidently there is also Hashem's help in the world!

The willow leaf has neither flavor nor fragrance, neither wisdom nor deeds. What then does it have—who needs it? It has the shape of a mouth; it is prayer. One who has nothing is praying all the time. As King David said, And I am prayer . . . (*Tehillim* 109:4) He constantly thought of himself as lacking and unworthy; therefore, he prayed all the time. The *Tehillim* which he authored are a testimony to the existence of Hashem's help. If there is a book full of prayer and yearning, then there is also one full of Hashem's assurance and help.

This was Yitzchak's blessing to Yaakov. "The voice is the

voice of Yaakov." (*Bereishis* 27:22) The redemption of
Yaakov, of the Jewish people, will come by the voice and by
their prayer. That is why *Mashiach*, the redeemer, (may he
soon come) will be a descendant of David.

The willow leaf, which we thought lowly and empty, is
really the one that ushers in the Age of Peace. Let us,
therefore, hold tightly those who seem empty, for it will be
their prayers that will bring the redemption to us and our
children.

❖

Sukkos is the time of the harvest. All summer long,
grain was growing in the field. Now it is cut, gathered,
threshed and piled in the storage place. It is the time when
a farmer measures his crop. During the months of the
summer, when the grain stood in the stalks, he might have
had an illusion about the size of his crop. However, now he
is able to break through the illusion. Now he sees how much
of the crop is chaff to be discarded, and how much is
precious food.

Similarly, after the powerful cleansing of *Yom Kippur*,
each of us can take stock of our state of affairs. It is harvest
time; time to take an honest look at how we fared during the
year. We take hold of the four *minim* as it is written, And
you shall take for yourselves . . . (*Vayikra* 23:40), which also
means, and you should take yourself. Each one of us should
take hold of ourselves and take a long, hard look at who we
are and where we are going.

❖

Sukkos is the time of harvest when the grain is gathered
into the house. We take the four types of plants from the

field into the *sukkah*, Hashem's shelter, and we rejoice there with Hashem.

A field is open to everyone's selfish hands and feet. A field is open to stealing and trampling. As it is written, For in the field, he did find the girl; she screamed for help, but there was no one to help her. (*Devarim* 22:27)

When we are out in the open field, when we have no direction, we can be blown away by the wind. As it is written, Not so are the evildoers; they are as the chaff that is blown away by the wind. (*Tehillim* 1:4) Those who are not yet in Hashem's shelter are easily blown by the wind and go to waste.

When we hold the four types of plants, we rejoice that we, no matter how lowly, are privileged to be in the *sukkah*. We have found our way to Hashem's protection, sheltered from dangerous winds.

———————— ❖ ————————

*T*he four *minim* are held as a prayer for water whose scarcity or abundance is judged during *Sukkos*. Water comes from the highest place as rain, and from the deepest place as brooks and wells. Its availability is tied to the prayers of the entire Jewish nation which can open mighty springs to supply everyone with water. This can only be if all of us, from the lowest to the highest, gather in holy unity. Therefore, just holding the plants together is already a prayer for water; for when we are together, the shower of blessings come, as it is written, Spring up, O well! Sing to it! The well which princes dug, which the nobles of the people delved, with the scepter and with their staves. (*Bamidbar* 21:18) These represent the four types of Jews: the princes are our three forefathers, who are symbolized by the myrtle branch having leaves of three covering the stem.

The nobles, who gave of themselves, are the willow branches who have but the yearning of their hearts to offer. The scepter, the lawgiver, is the *lulav* or palm, which has flavor or wisdom. Finally, the stave is the *esrog* or citron, for the stave is something on which one can lean and depend. It is the heart of man, a man with wisdom and good deeds. Thus, when we are joined together, we open the wellspring of blessing and the blessing of water flows abundantly.

———————— ❖ ————————

*T*he revelation of Hashem's kingdom in the world is Hashem's Name. Those who walk on the path of the Torah are writing Hashem's Name in the world. Likewise, those who break Hashem's laws erase His Name.

Each of the plants, the *esrog, lulav, haddas, aravah*, represents one of the four letters of Hashem's Name. By uniting with all four kinds of people we also accomplish the writing of Hashem's Name. This causes panic among the arrogant nations of the world. They claim to have their own power, independent of Hashem, and shudder at the thought that Hashem's Name will be revealed in the world. Therefore, the Jewish people who take hold of the four species of plants are hidden inside the *sukkah*. It protects them from the nations' enmity, for it is Hashem's shelter.

———————— ❖ ————————

*T*here are two abilities in man: wisdom, which resides in the mind, and actions, which emanate from the body. Without both of these he is incomplete and cannot function. If a man has wisdom but is unable to communicate, then what sort of man is he? If man is without the rudiments of human intellect, then, too, how can we speak of him as man? To fulfill Hashem's intention in the Creation, that we serve Hashem as human beings, we need both wisdom and physical activity.

These are represented by the two parts of the *tefillin*, one of which is tied on the head and the other on the upper part of the left arm. The *tefillin* worn on the head direct our wisdom toward Hashem; the *tefillin* on the arm direct our physical activity.

The holiday of *Sukkos* also has these two components. The *sukkah*, Hashem's shelter, is Hashem's Name, His wisdom, which flows to us in abundance and lovingkindness. How do we receive His wisdom? We must prepare vessels, and the vessel for wisdom is activity. Therefore, when we restore our activity during *Yom Kippur* by returning to Hashem, we then possess vessels for Hashem's lovingkindness of *Sukkos*.

Likewise, there are two components within our spiritual life. There is the voice of Yaakov and the hands of Esav. (*Bereishis* 27:22) The voice of Yaakov is the Torah and our yearning and prayers to live a Torah-directed life. We have the power to convert the hands of Esav into vessels for the voice of Yaakov. We can make physical activity a manifestation of the kingdom of Hashem.

This is the battle that occurs on *Yom Kippur*. The hands of Esav try to accuse the Jewish nation before the Heavenly Court. They present a great deal of evidence. "Look, the Jewish people are full of evil deeds," they say. However, despite the overwhelming accusations and evidence, we return to Hashem with all our heart and soul. We are not intimidated by our accusers, but we vigorously plead our case to Hashem. Finally, at the close of *Yom Kippur*, each one stands acquitted by the One and Only Judge of the Universe, who says, "I forgive; I purify." The hands of Esav are vanquished; the voice of Yaakov is victorious. Now the

Jewish nation has vessels to receive Hashem's wisdom. The hands of Esav are overwhelmed by the voice of Yaakov.

Yom Kippur's victory is symbolized by the *lulav*, a sword, and the other species are also likened to implements of war. The plants are a prayer for rain, i.e., Hashem's infinite Providence. Our prayers, the voice of Yaakov, were victorious against the hands of Esav.

When we enter the *sukkah* with the four species, we rejoice with Hashem in our victory to prepare vessels for the gift of wisdom. We stand completed with mind and body, and we turn to Hashem's shelter in order to stay in His house all the days of our life. (*Tehillim* 29:4) Then the *sukkah* becomes the protective tent of peace over us—peace, a sign to the end of striving. May we be worthy to experience such completion. Amen.

❖

*T*here are three realms: *olam*–space, *shanah*–time, and *nefesh*–life. Holiness of space was concentrated in the land of Israel, in the city of Yerushalayim, in the Beis Hamikdash. Holiness of time is concentrated in our holy days of *Shabbos* and the holidays. Holiness of life is concentrated in the pure soul which Hashem placed in each one of us.

The most powerful impact of holiness is at its beginning. Therefore, the first day of the holiday is most suitable for the performance of the *mitzvah* of *lulav*. (The Torah mentions specifically the taking of the *lulav* on the first day; later days are derived from a rabbinic ordinance. In the Beis Hamikdash the taking of the *lulav* all seven days was mandatory even before that ordinance.) When the holiness of time is at its greatest strength, the *lulav*, representing deeds, connects us to the root of blessing. The blessings of *Sukkos* shower upon us in abundance and without limit.

In the Beis Hamikdash, however, the holiness of space accompanies the holiness of time. Therefore, the *mitzvah* of *lulav* is performed there each of the seven days of *Sukkos*. When the Beis Hamikdash was destroyed, this custom ended, and the *mitzvah* of *lulav* was performed only the first day.

Rabbi Yochanan ben Zakai rectified this law and proclaimed that the *lulav* should be taken all the seven days even in the absence of the Beis Hamikdash. Although the Beis Hamikdash is absent in the physical realm of space, it is still present in the realm of life. The soul of the Jewish people always yearns for the Beis Hamikdash. As it is written, Our rejoicing was transformed to mourning. (*Eichah* 5:15) This means that what was previously accomplished by rejoicing is now equally done by mourning. The mourning, the emptiness of our hearts, sustains the spiritual being of the Beis Hamikdash among us. Therefore, we perform the *mitzvah* of *lulav* during the seven days of *Sukkos*.

The three realms of time, space and life are alluded to in the recitation of *Hallel*. (*Tehillim* 113-118) "Servants of Hashem, praise the Name of Hashem. May the Name of Hashem be praised for ever and ever." This is the realm of time. "From the east where the sun rises till where it sets, Hashem's Name is praised." This is the realm of space. "Hashem is most high upon all the nations." This is the realm of life.

As we hold the four plant species close to our hearts in the *sukkah*, remember, too, the Beis Hamikdash. The *sukkah* is also a temple of Hashem where Hashem's Name is holy and powerful. The heart is a holy temple where we yearn for the revelation of Hashem's kingdom. May we see this in our lifetime in the holy city of Yerushalayim before the eyes of all mankind.

*H*ashem's providence showers all creatures with infinite goodness. Each one, however, prepares differently to receive that goodness. Some only prepare containers for the material parts of Hashem's gifts. Some work harder and receive vitality on a spiritual level. Finally, those who are very fortunate receive the essence of the providence, the kernel or the soul and vitality of the goodness itself.

We can compare this to a king who invited his favorite servants to a party. After the royal feast, the king expressed how pleased he was with each of them and that they deserve to be rewarded. They were permitted to ask him for whatever they wished, except the crown and kingdom. The servants were overjoyed. Each one went off into a corner to decide his once-in-a-lifetime choice. Eventually, they were all ready. One asked for the royal chef and unlimited food. The other asked for the royal coach, horses and driver. The third asked for the royal baths. The last one said, "I ask for only a small favor. I want to marry the princess." The king smiled and said, "You have made the wisest of all choices. Whoever has the princess also has everything in the royal palace."

A similar incident happened when Shlomo first became king. In a dream, Hashem permitted him to ask for anything and it would be granted. Did he want riches, power, long life? Shlomo asked for wisdom. And Hashem said, "You have asked well. For whoever has wisdom has also everything else."

Likewise, the Jewish people ask for the essence, the kernel or the soul of Hashem's goodness. This is divine wisdom, Hashem's Name, the Torah and the soul in each one of us. It is the princess herself.

King Shlomo, who asked for wisdom, built the Beis Hamikdash, the small guest house, to receive Hashem's Divine Presence. The Jewish people who ask for the essence of providence, cleanse their hearts until they are fit dwelling places for Hashem Himself. This is symbolized by the *esrog*, that represents the heart, and the *lulav*, the Hebrew letters of which spell *lo lev*. We take the heart of wisdom, the princess, into the *sukkah*, the small guest house, in order to receive and to rejoice with Hashem.

❖

*T*here are *tzaddikim*, who walk on the path of Hashem constantly without any interruption, and there are *baalei teshuvah*, those who have stumbled but returned to Hashem. The *tzaddik* has chosen the straight and holy path, yet he is not without difficulties and setbacks. Each level he reaches is a new challenge to his righteousness and his commitment. Still, he struggles and persists, meeting each challenge and battling his difficulties. For example, suppose he chooses the holy path of kindness. Each time he is about to do a deed of kindness, he is confronted by unfavorable circumstances. Perhaps his kindness is socially unacceptable, being kind to a drunk or a vagabond on the street. Is someone truly making fun of the *tzaddik*, or is the opposition only in his mind? He does not know. Or he can choose very acceptable acts of kindness, lending sugar to a neighbor or aiding a dignified friend who is ill. Then he has no challenge. Therefore, the difficulties arise for the *tzaddik* only if his chosen path is challenged.

The *baal teshuvah*, the penitent, is different. In the past he has been confronted by every type of obstacle to the path of Hashem. He did not deal properly with all the challenges and confrontations. On the contrary, he floated with the current. On some level, he made each obstacle part of himself. When idols challenged his faith, he chose idols. When lust challenged his purity, he chose lust. When inertia challenged his good deeds, he chose not doing.

When he returns to Hashem, he brings with him all the challenges of his past. Thereby, he is elevated to a level even higher than the *tzaddik*. He comes face-to-face with Hashem in an instant.

It is written, The *tzaddik* will blossom as a date palm. (*Tehillim* 92:13) It takes a long time for the date palm to give fruit, and so does the *tzaddik*. But of the *baal teshuvah* it is written, And he will blossom as the rose. (*Hoshaya* 14:6) The rose opens its blossoms quickly, and so does the *baal teshuvah*.

Therefore, on *Sukkos* we take hold of the date palm and shake it vigorously. The trembling and shaking are the activity of a penitent attempting to reenter the palace of the king. The *baal teshuvah* is reaching the level of *tzaddik*. The rose is becoming a date blossom.

When we hold the *lulav* in the *sukkah*, Hashem's protective shelter, we bring to Hashem all our straying desires and actions, to consecrate them to the revelation of Hashem's kingdom.

❖

*T*he night before the Jewish people left Egypt, they were commanded to take branches from the *eizov* bush. (*Shemos* 12:22) The Talmud compares that taking to the verse, And you shall take for yourselves on the first day the fruit of a beautiful tree, branches of palm trees, and boughs of leafy trees and willows of the brook. (*Shemos* 23:40)

As slaves in Egypt, we were as low as the *eizov* bush. Hashem then lifted us to great heights. Moreover, Hashem desired that every generation, reach those heights by repentance and good deeds. This is the *lulav* which symbolizes our returning, our vigorous efforts to be with Hashem.

The redemption from Egypt was only caused by Hashem's great mercy. Only later through our persistent efforts did we become worthy of it. At first, we were received with kindness alone; later, we were received with strict judgment. Therefore, the kindness of *Sukkos* comes after the days of judgment of *Rosh Hashanah* and the forgiveness of *Yom Kippur*.

There are two ways to be bound to Hashem, one through kindness and mercy, the other through righteousness and judgment. As it is written, I will betroth you to me forever, I will betroth you to me with righteousness and judgment, kindness and mercy. (*Hoshaya* 2:19) We are at first bound to Hashem and brought close to him with humility. Although we have nothing and are undeserving, still Hashem redeems us. This is the *eizov* of the Exodus. Finally, we are tied to Hashem with judgment, repentance and good deeds. This is the *lulav* and the other *arba minim*.

❖

*H*ashem says, Return to Me and I will return to you. (*Zechariah* 1:3)

When a person sins, he loses part of his spiritual essence. If he repents and returns to Hashem, Hashem returns the power of his spiritual essence to him, as it is written, Take for yourselves on the first day . . . On *Sukkos*, each one of us can accept his inner spirituality in its full strength. This brings completeness and true joy to us. As it is written, Take . . . and you shall rejoice before Hashem your Lord seven days. (*Vayikra* 23:40)

Each one of the four species represents one of the four spiritual essences. When they are bound together, there is true joy. On *Shabbos*, when the realm of spiritual essences is united in the secret of the one (*Zohar, Tazria*), and all is one without divisiveness, there is no need for the *lulav*. The union is accomplished through the holiness of time, the *Shabbos*.

❖

*T*he willow leaf, the *aravah*, is shaped like a mouth, which symbolizes both prayer and Torah study. These are the inner secrets of the Jewish soul, as it is written, The voice is that of Yaakov. (*Bereishis* 27:22) This voice is the inner portion and kernel of holiness. The outer portion, the husk which protects it, is the fear of Hashem. He who is awed by the Creator focuses all his energies for an encounter with Him.

Torah and prayer are our greatest treasure, but they are stored in an inner sanctum. But the key to the outer doors is fear of Hashem, without which the treasure would soon be stolen. The outer doors are the fear of Hashem. (*Shabbos* 31b)

The Beis Hamikdash in Yerushalayim is the ultimate place of prayer in the world; for wherever a Jew is, he directs his prayers toward Yerushalayim. From Zion shall go forth the law and the word of Hashem from Yerushalayim. (*Yeshayahu* 2:3) It is the treasure house, yet it also is the outer gate where one can reach the highest level of fear of Hashem. Yerushalayim can be divided into two Hebrew words *yoreh shalem*, complete fear. In Yerushalayim, one can reach the ultimate level of fear of Hashem. He now has the inner and outer keys.

Therefore, we take the *aravah*, the willow, and shake it with the *lulav*. The four species tremble and pray together, "Hashem, the inner doors are always open for us, and so, too, is the depth of our soul. Please open the outer doors for us!" As it is written, Open up for me the gates of righteousness, let me enter through in them to praise Hashem. (*Tehillim* 18:19)

❖

*T*he *aravah* has neither flavor nor fragrance, and it symbolizes the individuals who have neither Torah wisdom nor good deeds. It is also symbolic of those generations that have no accomplishments, but who can only pray for Hashem's help. Of these it says, He turned to the prayer of the destitute, and he did not reject their prayers. (*Tehillim* 102:18)

Each plant represents a different type of person, and their survival is contingent on their unity. Each gives the other life and strength. As they give life horizontally to each other, they also give life vertically to the following generations. Thus, each generation gives strength to the next one, even to those who have nothing.

Our beliefs and customs link us to previous generations. We all have some Torah wisdom and good deeds, even if they are not our life goals and priorities. But we yearn that our customs of habit should become an essential part of us. And so we pray, "Please Hashem, may we be worthy to have our habits as our way of life." Therefore, the *aravah* is called a custom of the prophets.

We shake the four species, which includes the *aravah*, as a prayer. Even if we are empty of wisdom and good deeds, even if we are on the lowest level of habits, it links us to the illustrious people in this generation and previous ones.

❖

*T*he myrtle leaves, the *haddas*, have no flavor but a good fragrance. This is symbolic of those who have no

Torah wisdom yet possess good deeds. The triple leaves on each row of the branch symbolize our forefathers, Avraham, Yitzchak and Yaakov. Although they did not yet posses the Torah, they still did many good deeds.

What is the nature of this good fragrance? A fragrance can be detected far from its source. A fragrance also lingers after the source is gone. Like a prince who rebelled against the king and ran away from the palace dressed as a common person. When he passed a blind beggar, the beggar called out, "You come from the king's palace! I can never forget that fragrance! Who are you, pray tell me?"

Our forefathers blessed us that we should never lose the fragrance of the palace. The sweet scent comes from our past, and it also comes from our future. Every Jewish soul will experience the perfection of the World-to-Come. The future is this residual scent.

When we hold the *haddasim*, myrtle branches, we pray that their lovely fragrance should never leave us. Our good deeds should always be with us. It should not merely be a scent, but rooted in Torah wisdom, which constantly generates and gives forth the good fragrance.

9

THE DRAWING OF THE WATER

The water libation, how was it done? A golden flagon holding three lug of water was filled from the Pool of Shiloach. When they arrived at the Water Gate, they sounded a prolonged blast (tekiah), a quavering note (teruah) and a prolonged blast (tekiah). He went up the ramp and turned to his left where there were two silver bowls ... And they each had a hole like a narrow spout, one wide and the other narrow, so that both were emptied out together, the one to the west was for water, and that to the east was for wine. With one lug they could do the libations all the eight days.

(Sukkah 48a)

The sages have said that whoever has not seen the rejoicing at the celebration of the Simchas Beis Hasho'evah has never seen rejoicing in his life.

*At the close of the first day of the festival of Sukkos,
they went down to the Ezras Nashim where an
important rearrangement had been made. The golden
candlesticks were there with four golden bowls at
their tops and four ladders to each one, and four
young kohanim with pitchers of oil holding a
hundred and twenty lug in their hands, which they
used to pour into every bowl.*

*From the worn-out clothes and girdles of the
kohanim, they made wicks, and there was no courtyard in Yerushalayim that was not lit up from the
light at the Simchas Beis Hasho'evah.*

*Pious men and men of good deeds danced before
them with burning torches in their hands and sang
before them songs and praises. And the Levites on
harps, and on lyres, and with cymbals, and with
trumpets, and with other instruments of music
without number, upon the fifteen steps leading down
from the Ezras Yisrael to the Ezras Nashim, corresponding to the fifteen Songs of Ascent in the
Tehillim; upon them the Levites used to stand with
musical instruments and sing hymns.*

(Sukkah 51a)

*Rabbi Yehoshua the son of Chananiah said,
"When we rejoiced at the Simchas Beis Hasho'evah,
we did not sleep at all."*

(Sukkah 53a)

W hat was the great rejoicing when the water was
drawn from the well? It was because they drew with
it the holy spirit. (Sukkah 50b)
Joy is when a being is in harmony with itself and is totally

112

connected to its roots. Joy is the result of vitality and life; sadness comes from decline and death.

The holy spirit in man is the spirit of Hashem, as it is written, And He breathed into his nostrils a spirit of life. (*Bereishis* 2:7) When man was created, Hashem defined his being by breathing into him. Man's body is of this world, yet he has Hashem's breath within him. He stands, therefore, between Heaven and earth. His task is to combine these two spheres in order to be man. If he succeeds, he is then connected to his roots and is filled with vitality. If not, he is in danger of losing his life as a human being.

True joy comes from inner harmony, when every part of one's being is at home with the others. Artificial joy grows from outside. As it is written, And now take a musician and let him play for me, and the holy spirit will descend upon me. (*Melachim II* 3:15) This joy is empty, and the state of being empty is like a container. The container can be filled; one who is joyous is prepared to receive the holy spirit.

Therefore, those who rejoiced at the water drawing could not sleep at all. How can one sleep when one is constantly rising to new heights of life, vitality and total being? Let us also rejoice, so that the holy spirit may rest upon us.

❖

*Y*ou should rejoice in your holiday and you should be only joyous. (*Devarim* 16:14) Even when we have reasons not to be joyous, one should be only joyous. Even in the dark and dismal days of exile, when there seems to be nothing to celebrate, be only joyous! Especially on this night, the most joyous of all nights of the holiday.

❖

*A*nd He breathed into his nostrils a spirit of life, and man became a living being. (*Bereishis* 2:7) The *Targum* interprets this as, And man became a talking being. (*ibid.*)

Hashem's breath in man makes him what he is. Man can breathe out godly breath by speaking truth and words of Torah. The more he breathes out godliness, the more the breath of Hashem becomes part of him.

When a child is old enough to speak, the father teaches him to say, "The Torah was commanded to us by Moshe; an inheritance to the congregation of Yaakov." (*Devarim* 33:4) When a child starts to speak, he is defining himself as a human being. The breath of Hashem is being defined within his body. Immediately, we put the stamp of Hashem onto his breath by teaching him to say words of Torah.

This divine breath is also the source of prophecy. Even those who never reach a level of Biblical prophecy can still obtain some prophetic level. As the Talmud relates, The Jewish people, even if they are not prophets, are still the children of prophets. (*Pesachim* 66a) On some level each one of us, who breathes godly breath, is a prophet.

One who breathes godly breath is in touch with his inner spiritual self, there is true life and vitality—the greatest joy. On these nights we can touch our true source of the waters of life. Let Hashem's breath enter us and breathe out songs of praise to His holy Name.

---------------- ❖ ----------------

*A*nd the spirit of Hashem hovered over the water. (*Bereishis* 1:2)

The entire Creation is subordinated to Hashem, and Hashem's Spirit hovers over it. Who would not be happy with this situation? The one who is arrogant and wants his own independent power, who is not happy to serve Hashem and to follow His orders. Such a person falls into the clutches of like-minded people, and they enslave him. As it is written, Because you did not serve Hashem with joy and gladness . . . you will now serve your enemies. (*Devarim* 28:47)

The waters that are drawn on the nights of *Sukkos* bring our minds back to those waters which were in the world at the beginning of time, and we feel again Hashem's spirit hovering over us. This brings us the greatest joy. We are revitalized by this restoral of the earliest creation.

❖

*O*n *Yom Kippur*, the Jewish people are cleansed. This manifests that they are the ones chosen by Hashem to declare His kingdom. Likewise, it is clear that they have chosen Hashem as their ruler. This is the greatest of joys, for it is written, Hashem will rejoice in His creation (*Tehillim* 104:31), and Israel will rejoice in its Maker. (*Tehillim* 149:2)

When the Creator and the created become manifest, a song of joy rises to Heaven, as it is written, This nation I have formed for myself; they shall proclaim My praise. (*Yeshayahu* 43:21) When the forming of My people is clear, then My praise rises from the earth.

Yet the angels, too, praise the Creator. Whose songs of praise are sweeter?

We can compare this to a kind and just king whose servants rebelled and forced him to leave the palace. He disguised himself in rags and wandered in the city. He wandered among the poor and working classes, asking for food and lodging. He revealed his identity to many and asked for their help. He was pleased to hear their promises of loyalty. After many months, the king was certain that most of the citizens were loyal to him. The masses organized, and soon the king's cause captured the hearts of the entire province. The king sent word that he was ready to march on the palace. They amassed and approached the palace walls.

At that point, the king's ousted generals emerged from hiding and greeted the king, "Praised be the name of our kind and just king for ever and ever." They discussed strategy and organized the people for the assault. The citizens felt belittled. Now that the generals are here, they thought, we are not so important anymore! The king sensed their doubt and said, "If not for you, would my kingdom ever have become manifest?"

There is no sweeter praise than the Jewish nation singing of Hashem, the Creator of heaven and earth. There is no greater joy than the nights of *Sukkos* when this becomes clear before all of mankind.

❖

*A*t the celebration of drawing water in the Beis Hamikdash, Hillel would say, "If I am here, all is here." (*Sukkah* 53a)

The Jewish people are the vessels for the revelation of Hashem's kingdom. When they were in Yerushalayim, it was a thriving city and the Beis Hamikdash stood before all mankind. When they were exiled, the Beis Hamikdash together with Yerushalayim were destroyed. The kingdom of Hashem was concealed, and the light of the world was extinguished.

On the nights of *Sukkos*, our crucial role in the revelation of Hashem's kingdom becomes very clear to us. This is surely the greatest joy. As it is written, May our eyes see, and our hearts rejoice, and our spirits be gladdened in Your help when it will be told to Zion, "Behold! Your king reigns!" (*Tefillas Maariv*)

❖

*T*hey brought a pitcher of water and poured it onto the altar. As if Hashem is saying to them, "Pour the water before Me so that your yearly rain be blessed." (*Taanis* 2a)

Water is the essence of blessing both in the physical and spiritual sense. Every living thing is primarily water. Water helps things grow, thrive and flourish. However, rain can fall and go completely to waste. There must be containers in which to receive the rain.

When it rains, it rains on the righteous and evildoers alike. Therefore, on *Sukkos* there were offerings for all the seventy nations. Thus, all the nations benefit from the rain which falls on the Jewish people.

❖

*T*he grass of the field had not yet sprouted, for Hashem had not yet made it rain, and man was not yet there to work the land. (*Bereishis* 2:5)

When there are vessels to receive the divine blessing, the rain comes. Rain brings food and sustenance to all living things. Only man, who recognizes his Creator, can really appreciate the gift of rain, and recognize that at any time it might be withdrawn. Therefore, until the creation of man there was no rain.

The Jewish people desire rain for one reason. They want material well-being in order to serve Hashem without distractions. They fully recognize the true kindness of the gift of rain. Therefore, it is also Hashem's will that rain should fall only through the prayers of the Jewish people.

117

There are two ways that rain descends. It is written, He *gives* rain on the face of the land, and *sends* water on the outside streets. (*Iyov* 5:10) In the land of Israel, the vessel for all blessing that Hashem *gives* is rain. We are given this gift directly from the Hand of Hashem. Hashem *sends* the rain to other lands because His Hand is concealed there and they receive rain as if it came from a distant place.

When the Beis Hamikdash will stand again in Yerushalayim, Hashem will open for you His storehouse and give rain for your land in the proper season. (*Devarim* 28:12) But in a time of destruction and exile, the channel of gifts is indirect. Nevertheless, the divine gifts keep flowing with great kindness; and where there is sustenance, there is joy. The rejoicing of *Sukkos* is tied to the abundance of Hashem's gifts. Thus, we go to draw the holy waters from the wellsprings of help.

❖

*A*nd Hashem separated between the waters under the heavens and the waters upon the heavens. (*Bereishis* 1:7)

From then on there were upper waters and lower waters. The lower waters complained to Hashem, "We, too, want to be close to You. Why are we so far away?" (*Midrash Rabbah, Bereishis* 1:7) Hashem answered, "There will come a time when you, too, will be close, when your waters will be poured on the altar during the holiday of *Sukkos* to celebrate the drawing of the water." (*Tikunei Zohar* 5)

Man is composed of flesh and blood from the earth and a soul from Heaven. To help the soul dominate the body, he received the Torah whose teachings guide his life. If he lives according to the Torah, the divine aspect of his flesh and blood will be uncovered and thus create a new peace between heaven and earth.

On *Yom Kippur*, the Jewish people become pure as the angels of Heaven. This takes them directly into the *sukkah*, a tent of peace in which heaven and earth join together. This is the time to bridge the gap between the lower and upper waters. Just as the heavenly aspect of the earthly body has been revealed so can the heavenly aspect of the lower waters be raised up.

All of us who feel downtrodden, abandoned, frustrated and weak can take strength from the knowledge that it is within our power to raise lower waters to the heights of Heaven. Let us rejoice, celebrate and receive the refreshing waters of life and vitality for us, our children, all of Israel and all the nations of the world.

10

A TIME OF SUPPLICATION

What is the ritual of the willow branches? There was a place below Yerushalayim called Motsa. They went down there and collected young willow branches, and they came and set them upright along the sides of the altar with their tops bent over the top of the altar. They then sounded a long blast of the shofar (tekiah) and a quavering note (teruah) and a long blast (tekiah). Each day they walked in procession once around the altar and recited, "We beg you, Hashem, please help! We beg you, Hashem, please help us succeed!" (Tehillim 118:25) . . . But on the seventh day they walked in procession around the altar seven times.

(Sukkah 45a)

A nd he will kiss me from the kisses of his mouth . . . for your love is better than wine. (*Shir Hashirim* 1:2)

One can hold a child's hand, stroke his hair or hug him, and these are all signs of love. The mouth, however, is the essence of man. The mouth—speech—distinguishes man from animals. Our mouths are the voice of Yaakov. Kissing with the mouth is a meeting of the essence of two souls.

The connection of Hashem to the Jewish people is innate. The spiritual core of the inner soul is connected to the most infinite spiritual level which is Hashem.

Wine has both color and flavor, the fermented juice of grapes. Water is nothing but the essence of liquid. It is this water for which we pray on *Hoshanna Rabbah*, "Please, Hashem, help!" Therefore, we want the purest *aravah*, the willow branches which grow near water. This love, untouched by color or flavor, is a love of the inner soul. It is far superior to wine which contains the superficial attractions of appearance.

The willow leaves have neither taste nor fragrance, and they represent those of us who have neither Torah wisdom nor good deeds. We plead to Hashem, not on the strength of our good deeds, but because of the essential connection we have with Him, the kisses of His mouth.

There is still a further dimension. *Neshikah*, the Hebrew word for kiss, shares the root of the word *hashakah*. *Hashakah* is a legal term regarding two pools of water which are next to each other. One of the pools complies with all the laws of *mikveh*. The other pool contains water from a metal pump and is unfit for use as a *mikveh*. When there is an opening between the two pools and the water from one touches the water from the other, both can be used as a *mikveh*. When the waters touch each other, it is called *hashakah*, a kissing of the essences.

Though we are lacking in Torah wisdom and good deeds,

Hashem's essence is touching us. We are infused with holiness and purity. On *Hoshanna Rabbah* we plead, "Hashem, we are Your children. No matter what we do, we remain Your children. Please help us. Let us see Your kisses, Your constant love for us!"

❖

*O*n *Hoshanna Rabbah* we pray with the *aravah*, the willow branches. The *aravah* has neither flavor nor fragrance; it can only yearn and pray for help. The leaves are smooth and long; it is constantly praying. *Aravah* also means sweet. The voice of Yaakov is sweet to hear, for one who humbles himself has charm and finds favor in the eyes of his benefactor. *Aravah* also means to mix together. We are essentially mixed and united with Hashem. So we humbly plead to Hashem in a sweet voice from the depths of our hearts, for His help is surely coming.

❖

*M*an and beast alike will be helped by Hashem. (*Tehillim* 36:7) This verse refers to people who have the wisdom of man but consider themselves no higher than beasts. (*Chulin* 5b)

Human wisdom is full of delusion, as much as we know there is always someone who knows more, and beyond that the sum total of human knowledge is minute by comparison with the infinite knowledge of Hashem. True wisdom is the recognition of what we do not know. And so, on *Hoshanna Rabbah* we stand as beasts before their master, without power and little wisdom, just yearning for the help of Hashem.

*H*e turned to the prayer of the destitute, and He did not reject their prayer. (*Tehillim* 102:18)

The lowly, desolate and poor can only pray. He has nothing to claim as merit before his Master. But Hashem ignores all other prayers to listen to the prayer of the poor and lowly. The prayer of the others, filled with wisdom and good deeds, is accepted only together with the poor man's prayer.

A kingdom was struck by a fierce storm wreaking havoc and devastation upon rich and poor alike. Trees were uprooted; houses destroyed and fortunes lost. The people came to the king to plead for help. The rich came in first and cried to him about losing their mansions, orchards and thoroughbred horses which were all lost in the storm. The king had little sympathy for them. But when the poor people came in dressed in rags they did not know what to say. The storm took nothing from them; for they had nothing to take. They just gazed at the king and wept. Now the king felt the devastation of the storm, and he was ready to help all its victims.

The willow's leaf is shaped like a mouth. It pleads before Hashem, as it is written, As a line of scarlet are your lips, and your speech (*midbareich*) is beautiful. (*Shir Hashirim* 4:3) *Midbareich* means your desert. When you come to Hashem as a desert, empty and desolate, then your lips are beautiful.

On *Hoshanna Rabbah*, we stand as the poor beggar before the King. Then the divine kindness flows abundantly to a world so much in need of His help.

———————————— ❖ ————————————

*W*e use two branches of *aravah*. One represents the open lips of Moshe Rabbeinu. The other represents the closed lips of Aaron, as it is written, And Aaron was quiet.

(*Vayikra* 10:3) Moshe was the most humble individual on the face of the earth; however, he is not the one who brings peace and love among men. He is the teacher who imparts the teachings and the law of Hashem. It is the one who is quiet, receptive and accepting who can bring true peace. Aaron is called the one who loved peace and pursued peace. (*Avos* 1:12)

Similarly, to speak evil, to argue, to cause dissension and to hate are the worst of sins. They rend asunder and destroy. Therefore, one who is quiet at such times upholds the entire world. His power is great and infinite.

Ultimately, one is dependent on the other. To the degree that one is able to hold his lips together, that is how well he can open them. The quiet one then can speak the words of law. For it is written, As the kiss of lips, so is he who answers properly. (*Mishlei* 24:26) One whose lips are kissed together in quiet is worthy to answer properly.

The *aravah* that is tied to the *lulav* with the other species is the open lips. It is connected with those who have Torah wisdom, and it participates with them. The *aravah* of *Hoshanna Rabbah* is the quiet one who has nothing to say but yearns for the help of Hashem and the complete redemption.

---❖---

*T*he willow leaf is smooth-edged; it has no raised parts. It is a pure and empty vessel to receive the blessing of Hashem. It symbolizes the one who has nothing and can only pray. As David Hamelech said of himself, And I am prayer. (*Tehillim* 109:4) That is to say, I can do nothing but pray before Hashem.

Taking the *aravah* on *Hoshanna Rabbah* is called a custom of the prophets. (*Sukkah* 44a)

The connection that Hashem has with the Jewish people is heart-to-heart, for it is one of essence. The Jewish people are all prophets, and their customs grow out of their relationship with Hashem.

The nations of the world can ignore our chosenness when it is based on good deeds. It is natural that as you sow you also reap. However, when they feel that our relationship with Hashem is deeper than that created by our good deeds they are overwhelmed by hatred. They oppose the *aravah*, the willow that is without flavor or fragrance, for it is special in the eyes of Hashem. For this opposition alone, we need help. Hashem should protect us from their jealousy.

In our present exile, the designation of chosen people is an embarrassment to us. What an irony! Hashem's kingdom is concealed, and we are downtrodden, and yet they hate us for being the chosen nation? But there will come a day when this will change, for it is written, I will find you in the market place; I will kiss you; still they will not shame Me. (*Shir Hashirim* 8:1) I will kiss you, symbolizes the relationship of the inner spirit. And we will not be ashamed, for Hashem's kingdom will be revealed to all.

On *Hoshanna Rabbah*, we come to Hashem as prophets who understand each other's heart. We all need the redemption . . . for our sake . . . for Your sake.

❖

*T*he four species each represent a component of the Torah. The *lulav* has only flavor; that is Torah wisdom. The *haddas* has only fragrance; that is *mitzvah* or deeds. The *esrogim* with flavor and fragrance are *mishpatim*, laws with logical reason. The *aravos* with neither taste nor fragrance, are the *chukim*, laws with reasons incomprehensible to the human mind.

Likewise, there are four components in evil. There are the four exiles of Babylon, Persia, Media and the present Edom. And there are the four most severe transgressions: idol worship, incest, murder and hatred without cause. These are linked in that order, and the present exile is related to hatred without cause.

Why are we in exile? Because we lack faith in Hashem's love for us. We excuse ourselves on the grounds that we are not worthy, but He loves us even if we are empty of flavor and fragrance.

Why do we hate? Because another person has neither flavor nor fragrance. If we accepted that Hashem's love for us is even without flavor or fragrance, we would not hate; and that is why we are in exile.

But on *Hoshanna Rabbah*, we can restore our faith in Hashem's love for the Jewish people. We hold tightly the *aravah* with great love, even if it has neither flavor nor fragrance. We pray to Hashem, We are all empty vessels ready to receive Your divine providence. We stand together with all the people regardless of their emptiness. This is the way You love us, Hashem. Now, please redeem us, your lowly ones, from exile.

———————— ❖ ————————

*H*oshanna Rabbah is the last day of *Sukkos* which symbolizes David Hamelech. The sprouting of Your servant, David, You should bring forth speedily in our days. (*Shemoneh Esrei*) We pray and yearn with the *aravah* for the Redemption that should come in our days.

———————— ❖ ————————

*D*uring all of *Sukkos*, we keep the four species together, those that have Torah wisdom and good deeds with even those who have neither one. We are then in the *sukkah*, the house of Hashem, and we are able to unite. At the end of *Sukkos* we feel the impact of our exile, which originated with the destruction of the Second Beis Hamikdash in Yerushalayim. The hatred which caused that destruction still haunts us today and does not allow us to hold the four species together. We, therefore, hold the *aravah* which is now separated from the *lulav*.

What can we do to escape exile's curse? Remembering our own insignificance, and the way we resemble the *aravah* without flavor or fragrance, and then taking the *aravah* on *Hoshanna Rabbah* and lowering it to the ground. We strike it on the ground again and again, and the sound of that beating is a prayer. "Please, Hashem, even if we are only as the *aravah*, so bare and lowly, listen to our prayer. Even if we cannot unite with the rest of Israel because of the exile, help us! See our humility! We know we are truly empty. Redeem us quickly for Your sake."

❖

I was poor and He helped me. (*Tehillim* 116:6) It is because we realize our poverty that Hashem helps us, as it is written, Not because you are more numerous than the other nations . . . you are but the minutest of all nations. (*Devarim* 7:7) Because you humble yourselves more than the other nations, therefore, you are a vessel to receive Hashem's providence.

There are some, however, who use humility itself as a source of arrogance. It is used as a social ladder in order to climb higher than others. This is why serrated willow leaves are not to be used. The humility must be smooth, for one must subordinate one's self to those who are better and higher.

On *Hoshanna Rabbah*, we humble ourselves in order to become vessels to receive *hoshanna*, the help from Hashem. The lower we are, the more likely is our redemption, which we hope and pray will soon come in our days.

❖

*T*he Jewish people were blessed with the virtue of poverty and humility. It is this virtue of humility which makes the Jewish people vessels for all of Hashem's gifts, as it is written, May water flow forth from his pails (*dalyav*). (*Bamidbar* 24:7) *Dalyav* also means the poor ones. The water of life, the Torah, will flow from those who are poor. They are proper vessels to receive the gift of wisdom. Therefore, we take the lowly willow leaves which grow near the water. Flowing water represents the abundance of Hashem's gifts. Those who lower themselves properly are recipients of it. This is the message of *Hoshanna Rabbah*, the great help on this last day of *Sukkos*. We resign ourselves to the wonderful Jewish virtue of humility and prepare for the redemption.

❖

*T*he *aravah* has neither wisdom nor good deeds. Then in what way is it connected to Hashem? With faith. The leaves are smooth and flowing. Our hearts yearn and flow; they follow Hashem even into the desert, as it is written, Draw me to follow you and I will run. (*Shir Hashirim* 1:4) We follow Hashem as an animal led by its master.

We can compare this to a king who had one son and many servants. They all lived in the palace, enjoying the benefits of royalty. Then tragedies befell the kingdom. Famine was followed by war and pestilence. Little by little, the servants abandoned the king. Soon, there was hardly a loyal servant left except the king's son. He was asked, "Why do you stay with the king after all these tragic events?"

"Why do I stay with the king?" he answered. "The king is my father!"

A son inherits from his father on two levels. On one level, he receives wisdom. On the lower level, the son is the footstep, or knee, of his father. (*Eruvin* 70b) The son follows his father and walks in his footsteps. This is beyond understanding, sense or logic. It is faith alone.

Parents teach their children with elaborate explanations. There are some things for which they neither give rhyme nor reason. The children experience neither flavor nor fragrance, yet they follow the customs of their parents.

This is the level of *aravah*, the lowly willow—pure faith. Therefore, the *aravah*, which we clasp on *Hoshanna Rabbah*, is but a custom from the days of the prophets. (*Sukkah* 44a) Customs and faith go hand in hand.

It is written, If you do not know the beautiful one among the women, go therefore to the footsteps of the sheep. (*Shir Hashirim* 1:8) If you are not positive which among the nations belongs to Hashem, go and see their footsteps. Who walks in Hashem's path with pure faith when all have abandoned Him because of difficulties?

When we left Egypt, before we had flavor or fragrance, we already followed Hashem with pure faith. And our future redemption will come through faith although we are lowly as the willow.

❖

*T*he willow, without flavor or fragrance, symbolizes the Jewish people. They know truly that only Hashem possesses power and all the gifts one may need. They know also that they are not chosen due to any merit, but their chosenness comes from an essential relationship with Hashem, as it is written, And I have planted you as a noble vine; all are true seed. (*Yirmiyahu* 2:21) As a seed is related to the tree, so is the Jewish people related to Hashem.

Although people can choose whether to be truthful or to live lives of deceit and falsehood, they cannot falsify seed; each tree will only sprout its own seed. The Hebrew letters of *aravah* have the same numerical value as *zera*, seed. The *aravah* represents truth, for a seed is truth.

The Chozeh of Lublin once said, "If someone feels no connection with Hashem, it may be because he realizes the scope of his inadequacies, that he possesses neither Torah wisdom nor good deeds. This is the truth—and he is therefore in fact connected to Hashem, the God of Truth."

❖

*T*he *aravah* grows by the water, as it is written, Willows of the brook. (*Vayikra* 23:40) The Hebrew letters of *nachal*, brook, are an acrostic for the words *nafsheinu chiksah Lashem*, our souls yearn for Hashem. (*Tehillim* 33:20) The yearning of our hearts opens the source of water, the waters of help.

We are like the willow, thirsting for water, yet unfulfilled by all the waters in the world. Our thirst remains unquenched until we drink the purest of all waters, the waters of Torah.

This was implicit in Yaakov's blessing to Yosef's children. Let them multiply as the fish in the midst of the land. (*Bereishis* 28:16) Fish, who live in water, are constantly thirsty for water. The Jewish people should never be satisfied until they obtain the purest water. Let them be like the parched, dry land; no matter how much water it has to drink, it is not satisfied until the purest water comes.

On *Hoshanna Rabbah*, we are thirsty for the purest water, let our souls yearn for Hashem alone.

❖

*F*or in the field, he did find the girl; she screamed for help, but there was no one to help her. (*Devarim* 22:27) If one does hear her pleas for help, he may take the attacker's life. (*Sanhedrin* 73a)

Our enemy, the power of evil in this world, attacks us. We scream and plead for Hashem's help. Why does He not take the life of the attacker? Why does He not erase evil from our midst? The answer is in the field, the field of aimlessness and desolate emptiness. We have exposed ourselves to evil; how can we ask Hashem to kill the evil?

On *Yom Kippur*, however, we become pure and focus our lives toward Hashem. Now if we scream He will answer us. So we cry on *Hoshanna Rabbah*, "Please, Hashem, once and for all, remove the evil from among us! Redeem us totally and finally for the sake of Your holy Name!"

11

THE EXTRA HOLIDAY

On the eighth day, you shall have a solemn assembly; you shall do no laborious work, but you shall offer a burnt offering, an offering by fire, a pleasant fragrance to Hashem.

(Bamidbar 29:35)

The divine control of the world is hidden by nature. Everything appears to operate according to natural laws. During *Sukkos* the Jewish people have a strong experience of the spiritual nature of the world. This experience is in contravention to the apparent nature of the world, and it is protected inside the *sukkah*.

But the eighth day, *Shemini Atzeress*, is beyond the seven days of creation, and therefore beyond nature. It is actually a day from the World-to-Come where there is no need for concealment.

The divine nature of the world is also revealed through Torah—the Word of Hashem. The Torah teaches each person what to do for Hashem in this world. Therefore, the Torah is celebrated on *Shemini Atzeress*.

During the seven days of *Sukkos*, we make offerings for all the seventy nations. However, on the eighth day, only one offering is made. This offering is only for the Jewish nation. On this day, the relationship between Hashem and the Jewish people is clear. The divine reality needs no protection; consequently, we do not sit in the *sukkah*.

❖

*O*n the eighth day, you shall have a solemn assembly. (*Bamidbar* 29:35) The Talmud compares this to a king who made a celebration for his trusted subjects. There were seven days of royal feasts and lavish entertainment. When it was over, the subjects were preparing to leave. The king said to them, "It is very hard for me to part with you. Please prepare a simple dinner so that we can sit as friends and enjoy each other's company." (*Sukkah* 55b)

Hashem's kindness to all the nations is constant and generous, more than they are equipped to handle—this is symbolized by the seventy sacrifices offered on *Sukkos* as we are judged for rain. But on the eighth day, there is a private feast just for Klal Yisrael. Only one sacrifice honors our private day of celebration, as we finally pray for *geshem*, steady rain which is poured on the world when we merit it.

❖

*O*n the eighth day, you shall have a solemn assembly. (*Bamidbar* 29:35) We could understand this to mean that on the eighth day, one can feel a sense of gathering, a sense of how small and insignificant the individual is and that the only strength he receives is from Hashem.

The Baal Shem Tov said, "A man comes in from the cold winter air to warm himself by the blazing fireplace. Soon, his clothes and skin thaw and start to warm. Then he becomes warmer until he is too hot to stand close by the flames. He moves back where there is less heat. Soon, his body cools, and again he draws near the fire. This, too, is our relationship with Hashem. Too close, you can burn; too far, you freeze. You are constantly going nearer and further, as the prophet says, And the celestial creatures run forth and back. (*Yechezkel* 1:14)"

Every time we realize our own unworthiness, Hashem's warmth enters us. During the holiday of *Sukkos*, we receive an abundance of gifts; and humble ourselves totally. As a result, we receive the holiday of *Shemini Atzeress* which is divine beyond any limitations.

❖

We move from our homes into the *sukkah*, Hashem's shelter. On the eighth day, we return to our homes with the gifts that we received in the *sukkah*. What gifts did we receive? On a simple level, each of us received renewed strength, vitality and faith. On a more complex level, the gift was the very fact of our staying in the house of Hashem and our refusal to leave it for seven days. This is the greatest gift of all; Hashem permitted us to draw closer to Him.

❖

The *Zohar* relates that there are two types of *baalei teshuvah*. One feels badly about the evil he had done, and he repents out of remorse. The more complete form of *teshuvah* is motivated just by a longing to seek Hashem. Transgressions block the desire to seek Hashem, and *teshuvah* is the restoral of that desire.

Sukkos is marked by rejoicing that Hashem has forgiven our sins. We are now cleansed of the troublesome deeds of our past. But on *Shemini Atzeress*, the rejoicing is deeper; we feel that Hashem allowed us to seek Him again.

❖

*T*he *Mishnah* in *Avos* teaches us that there are three crowns: royalty, Torah and priesthood. Each corresponds to one of the three holidays. *Pesach*, when we left Egypt and became a nation and Hashem became our king, relates to the crown of royalty. *Shavuos*, when we received the Torah at Mount Sinai, relates to the crown of Torah. *Sukkos*, the reminder of the clouds of glory, which came in the merit of Aaron the Kohein, relates to the crown of priesthood.

However, the *Mishnah* concludes, The crown of a good name is higher than all of them. (*Avos* 4:17) The three holidays are divine gifts, but *Shemini Atzeress* is a result of what we have accomplished by our own deeds. *Shemini Atzeress* is the crown of a good name.

The three patriarchs, Avraham, Yitzchak and Yaakov, provided a firm base for the Jewish people, but there was still a need for another founder—David Hamelech. His descendant will be *Mashiach*, who will redeem and end all exiles forever and usher in an era of true peace and tranquility.

The last day of *Sukkos* symbolizes that epoch, the dynasty of David Hamelech and the arrival of *Mashiach*. Our celebration of *Shemini Atzeress* relates to that period, the era of peace—the crown of a good name for the whole Jewish nation.

*W*hen Shlomo Hamelech finished building the Beis Hamikdash in Yerushalayim, he made a celebration for seven days. On the eighth day, he sent everyone home. (*Melachim I* 8:66)

During *Sukkos*, all the seventy nations receive gifts of divine blessing, but on the eighth day, the nations take their leave; they collect their gifts and run. But the king's family accompanies him to his chambers. When they receive their gifts, it reminds them how much they want to be with him. Hashem's presence is above and beyond the material world. It is beyond the seven days of creation; it is already eight. That is why we stay on to celebrate *Shemini Atzeress*.

❖

*T*he kingdom of Heaven is concealed in this world. Therefore, the close relationship between the Creator and His people is also concealed. It is the task of the Jewish people to reveal it. During each holiday, some aspect of this special relationship becomes revealed. *Shemini Atzeress* is the last of the year's holidays. It is the final revelation.

On *Rosh Hashanah* the lovingkindness of Hashem is hidden, and all the world is in judgment. It seems as if the world will be destroyed, for surely no one is worthy, as it is written, Sound the *shofar* on the New Moon in the concealment of our holiday. (*Tehillim* 81:4) This forces the Jewish people to work hard at prayer and good deeds and then work constantly for twenty-one days. Finally, it is the eighth day, *Shemini Atzeress*, and Hashem's Name is clearly manifest in the world.

One Name of Hashem is spelled: *alef, hay, yud, hay*, and has the numerical value of twenty-one. These are the twenty-one days that the Jewish nation toils to reveal Hashem's kingdom, the World-to-Come—the days of *Mashiach*.

We are also taught, You should rejoice in your holiday, and you should be only joyous. (*Devarim* 16:14) The Hebrew word for only is *ach*, which is spelled *alef, chaf*; it also has the numerical equivalent of twenty-one. When you work twenty-one days, from the concealment of *Rosh Hashanah* till the revelation of *Shemini Atzeress*, then you are worthy of only happiness in its simplest purity.

Sukkos is called the time of gathering; the energies of the year are gathered to serve Hashem. This exposes us to danger from the evil powers, and Hashem takes us into the *sukkah* to protect us.

Shabbos is also a time for gathering the energy of the entire week and dedicating it for the divine purpose in Creation. So *Shabbos* is also given a tent of peace that is spread over us, as we recite in the *Shabbos* evening prayers, He who spreads His tent of peace over us and all of Israel and Yerushalayim.

On the twenty-first day, we have arrived at a dimension of time which is beyond time. It is the time of I-will-be—but is not yet to be—the World-to-Come.

Many of the greatest *tzaddikim* yearned to taste the World-to-Come. How would that infinite joy taste? How peaceful is divine peace? And here is a day of the World-to-Come to taste! Those who taste it are lifted to ecstatic heights beyond normal time and space. They sing and dance in joy while expressing the pure sense of peace within their souls.

———————— ❖ ————————

*T*he holiday of *Sukkos* is finished, yet the Jewish people add another day of celebration. This is *Shemini Atzeress*.

When a person travels and sees the beautiful culture of a faraway place he will bring back mementoes, to bring the taste of his travels back to his own home. Similarly, when we leave *Shabbos*, we take some of it into the following week by adding several minutes onto the *Shabbos*. When on *Shemini Atzeress* we leave the holy season behind us, we take some of the holiness of the *sukkah* into our year round abode.

❖

*E*ach of the holidays has special *mitzvos* associated with it. *Pesach* has *matzah*; *Shavuos* has the *shtei halachem*, two-loaf offerings; *Sukkos* has the *sukkah*. But *Shemini Atzeress* has nothing but the concept that you should be only joyous. (*Devarim* 16:15) We no longer need to convert some material objects to spiritual use, but can proceed directly to spiritual pleasure.

❖

*T*he world was created with the Hebrew letter *hay*, the softest and easiest sound in the alphabet. There was just a breath—and the world was there. The letter *hay* has a large opening below and a small opening near the top. This symbolizes that if a person wants to abandon his special mission and fall lower, he has plenty of room. However, he can still return, although with much greater difficulty, through the small opening at top.

Similarly, a halachically or technically valid *sukkah* needs two complete walls and one partial wall. This is the same shape as the *hay*, therefore, it is the shelter of the penitent.

Likewise, it is written, His hand is open to accept those who return. (*Yom Kippur Tefillos*) The Hebrew word for hand is *yad*, which is composed of the two Hebrew letters, *yud* and *daled*. Both letters together form the shape of the letter *hay*, the symbol of *teshuvah*.

138

Hashem opens a door for *teshuvah* with His great mercy and kindness. We open a door to Him through yearning and prayer. The door which Hashem opens for us is constantly open, and its opening is infinite; it is like the sea, always open. The door which we open with yearning and prayer is like a *mikveh*, a ritual bath, sometimes open and sometimes closed. (*Midrash Rabbah, Eichah* 3:34) There are special conditions which validate a *mikveh*. If the conditions are not met, the *mikveh* is not open. Similarly, if our hearts are not prepared properly for Hashem, then our door is not open.

On *Sukkos*, all of mankind may enter if they so desire. On the eighth day, the door of yearning and prayer is opened only for the Jewish nation. They gather together to pour out their hearts before Hashem, and they beg for rain, that the divine gifts should come to them. The limited opening of our hearts becomes infinite and our path is clear.

❖

Sukkos is the festival when the Jewish people gather for blessing and peace. Their gathering also ends with peace, as it is written, On the eighth day, you shall have a solemn assembly. (*Bamidbar* 29:35) On the other hand, the arrogant evildoers gather to do evil. Evil is separation, fragmentation, the opposite of peace.

❖

*O*ne of the Names of Hashem is *Sha-dai*—He who said, "Enough!" to His world. (*Midrash Rabbah, Bereishis* 1:1)

Where was the world spreading? On a simple level, it was spreading deeper and deeper into materialism. At first, the divine nature of creation was crystal clear, because it was very close to its divine roots. Then, as it spread, it moved deeper into the world of illusion.

The mission of the Jewish nation is to reiterate the original command of, "Enough!" It is to reestablish the divine nature of the world and to reveal its true roots. This is done on *Sukkos* on an elementary level. It is the time of gathering, particularly on the eighth day, a day of solemn assembly. The name *Atzeress* signifies its special blessing of holding us and our purpose together. The Torah is the ultimate revelation of divine roots in the world. Thus, the eighth day is also the rejoicing of the Torah.

❖

*S*ix days you should eat *matzos*, and the seventh is a day of solemn assembly. (*Devarim* 16:8)

When the Jewish people left Egypt, the Egyptian army chased them to the Red Sea. Miraculously, they were saved on the seventh day. For six days, it was still *matzos* which also means *mitzah*, quarrel and conflict. On the seventh day, they were finally assembled in total freedom.

Similarly, throughout *Sukkos*, the Jewish nation is still in battle. The battle started with the judgment of *Rosh Hashanah*, the New Year. They are judged together with the entire world. The battle is, who will be vindicated? On *Yom Kippur*, the battle enters a new phase. The Jewish people clamor for the acceptance of their purification. Finally, on *Sukkos* they enter Hashem's shelter, yet there is still room for the other nations and offerings are made for the seventy nations of the world. On *Shemini Atzeress*, all is quiet. The battle is won. We are totally assembled in peace.

❖

*Y*ou should celebrate the holiday for seven days. The first day is a rest day, and the eighth day shall be a solemn rest. (*Vayikra* 23:39)

The seven days of *Sukkos* represent the material world. The material world is made up of fragments, and we assign numbers to these fragments. However, the number eight represents the divine nature of the world. It is not an ordinary number but a singularity; therefore, the eighth day unifies all the seven days that passed.

The nations of the world all have the ambition to rule the world. Their actions are divisive and fragmenting. Therefore, offerings are made on *Sukkos* for them all. Their connection is with the fragmented numbers of the seven days. But the eighth day is unity and true peace. This day is reserved for the Jewish nation who yearn and pray, hope and make the world a place where . . . nation shall not lift sword against nation, neither will they know war any more. (*Yeshayahu* 2:4)

❖

*A*nd Moshe declared to the people of Israel the feast days of Hashem. (*Vayikra* 23:39)

Each of the holidays brings a special blessing to the Jewish nation. These blessings come in the merit of our forefathers Avraham, Yitzchak and Yaakov. The blessing could come, but how are they received? This was accomplished by Moshe. He connected the holidays to the heart and soul of the Jewish people.

Moshe was totally saturated with Torah energy. The Torah that he taught instructs us how to receive those teachings. Therefore, Moshe's declaration of the holidays opened the Jewish people's hearts to receive Hashem's bountiful gifts. This was and is the uniqueness of *Shemini*

Atzeress; it opens our hearts to receive the blessings of the other holidays.

---------------------- ❖ ----------------------

*O*n the eighth day, you shall have a solemn assembly. (*Bamidbar* 29:35)

When people unite for the sake of Hashem, the unity remains even after the project is completed. *Sukkos* is the time of gathering, but its unity remains through the eighth day, thus retaining the unity of *Sukkos* for the whole year.

12

PRAYING FOR RAIN

From when should one mention the power of rain?
Rabbi Eliezer says, "From the first day of the
festival of Sukkos." Rabbi Yehoshua says, "From the
last day of the Sukkos. Said Rabbi Yehoshua to him,
"Since rain during the holiday is but a sign of a
curse, why should one make mention of it?" Rabbi
Eliezer replied to him, "I did not really say to pray
for, but merely to mention the One who causes the
wind to blow and the rain to fall in its proper
season." He answered him, "If so, one should
mention it at all times."

(Taanis 2a)

(The opinion of Rabbi Yehoshua is accepted.)

The world was created on *Rosh Hashanah*, and then we
recite, "This is the day You have started to make the
world." (*Rosh Hashanah Tefillos*) It was formed and shaped

according to enduring natural laws. Man also is part of this creation, and it is for him to look after Hashem's work. Therefore, before man there was no rain; Hashem did not yet bring rain on the earth as there was no man to work the soil. (*Bereishis* 2:5) When man was created, he looked around and realized that the earth needed rain. He yearned and prayed. The rain came.

When you are positive something will happen, you do not pray for it. When there is doubt, then there is also yearning and prayer. Rain is always uncertain. Therefore, when man looked at the parched earth, he prayed for rain. In order to pray, we must step beyond the certainties in our hearts and evaluate our needs. We need rain, the blessings of Hashem, the holy Torah.

❖

*T*he three holidays, *Pesach*, *Shavuos* and *Sukkos*, correspond to the three blessings we all need: children, life and sustenance. *Pesach* is for children, to whom we retell the story of our Exodus. *Shavuos* is the day when the Torah was given; the Torah is our life. Finally, *Sukkos* is the time when we beg for rain, sustenance from our Creator.

This is a time of joy, and Hashem is happy to provide for His creatures. Similarly, we too should provide sustenance to others. This brings even more blessing from Hashem's treasury, which is open to our bodies and our souls.

❖

*A*nd from *midbar* [they came] to Matanah. (*Bamidbar* 21:18) This could be translated as "from the desert to the gift," since the Hebrew word for gift is *matanah*. It teaches us that one who makes himself open as the desert is ready

144

to receive Hashem's gift. In the desert, a brook of fresh water followed the Jewish people constantly. Likewise, if we make ourselves as a desert we shall receive water.

During each of the three holidays, the wellspring of Hashem's gifts is opened. On *Pesach* and *Shavuos*, this well is partially manifest, more so on *Sukkos*, and totally on *Shemini Atzeress*.

❖

*W*hen they came to Marah, they could not drink the water of Marah because it was bitter . . . and Hashem showed him a tree, and he threw it into the water and the water became sweet . . . Then they came to Elim, where there were twelve springs of water and seventy palm trees; and they encamped by the water. (*Shemos* 15:23-27)

Hashem's gifts of water flow through the twelve springs, the twelve tribes. By way of many channels, the seventy nations of the world receive sustenance, too. The work of the Jewish nation is to sweeten the water and stop it from going to waste. When we pray for rain, let us purify our hearts and have the proper vessels for the gifts which Hashem gives us in abundance.

❖

*I*n Eretz Yisrael the water, or rainy season, starts after *Sukkos*. The summer begins with *Pesach*. During the rainy season, the farmer does not work. He prays and watches the rain vitalize his fields. Most of his work is done during the summer.

Similarly, in spiritual matters, most of the worship in the Beis Hamikdash took place during the summer months during the three major holidays. The rainy season contains the potential which becomes actualized in the summer. When we complete our work, Hashem starts His, and therefore, on *Shemini Atzeress* we pray for rain.

❖

*P*our before me water during your feast day in order that the rain for the year will be blessed. (*Taanis* 2a)

When Hashem created the Heavens, He separated the upper waters and the lower waters. The lower waters cried constantly that they want to be near Hashem. In turn, Hashem promised to have them poured on the altar and to offer salt with the sacrifices. (*Tikunei Zohar* 5)

The separation of the lower waters and their distance from Hashem is an illusion. All water is equally close to the Creator. And there is no preparation of the water; it is poured on the altar in its natural state. This shows that water, no matter if it is higher or lower, is close to Hashem.

Wine, on the other hand, requires much effort before it can be offered on the altar. Grapes are cut, pressed, strained and filtered. Water is pure and acceptable as is; therefore, Hashem allows the lofty nature of the lower waters to be revealed during *Sukkos*. This happens during the ceremony of pouring the water on the altar.

Our prayer on the eighth day is not just for rain, we are yearning for the revelation of Hashem in the world.

❖

*T*he strength of rain is mentioned . . . [in the second part of the *Shemoneh Esrei*]. Why the word "strength"? Because it falls with strength. (*Taanis* 2a)

Each and every creature in the world receives sustenance from Hashem. Everyone benefits from Hashem's bounty, but some are entitled to their sustenance by right.

Hashem's sustenance comes to the Jewish people according to justice, not just according to the rules of kindness, as it is written, He turns the rock into a pool of water, the flint into a spring of water. (*Tehillim* 114:8) Even the rock, the strictness of judgment, is turned into flowing kindness. It is also written, You open Your Hand and satisfy the desire of every living thing. (*Tehillim* 134:16) Hand always refers to the left hand, which symbolizes strict judgment. Nevertheless, for those who deserve, even the left hand is open and satisfies their desires.

On the eighth day, *Shemini Atzeress*, it finally becomes clear who deserves sustenance. We stand before Hashem as His children and receive from His open Hand.

13

REJOICING WITH THE TORAH

*On the eighth day, Shemini Atzeress, it is custom-
ary to make a celebration with the Torah. Outside of
Eretz Yisrael, it is celebrated on the ninth day, which
is commonly called Simchas Torah.*

*The chassidic masters developed the custom of
celebrating with the Torah both on Shemini Atzeress,
as in Eretz Yisrael, and on the next day of Simchas
Torah.*

Two kinds of happiness are derived from Torah. One is
the result of learning something new, and is relative to
the clarity of understanding. The other stems from the
mere fact of receiving the Word of Hashem.

The Talmud teaches us the following interpretation: The
Torah was commanded to us by Moshe; an inheritance—
morashah—to the congregation of Yaakov. (*Devarim* 33:4)
Do not read the word as *morashah*—an inheritance, but

meorasah—betrothed. To learn Torah one must seek to be betrothed to the Word of Hashem. One must try to know the Torah like a wife, rejoicing in every revealed and hidden meaning and interpretation.

The deeper level is *morasha*, an inheritance. Not everyone can connect with this inheritance. All of Israel shares this inheritance, and only by subjugating oneself to the whole community of Israel can the deeper part of Torah be inherited. The eighth day is an *atzeress*, a gathering day, for all Israel when we can lay claim to our portion of the Torah heritage.

❖

*T*he rejoicing with the Torah is at the beginning of the year. The joy, singing and dancing opens our hearts and makes us yearn for a life filled with Torah. Even before the Torah enters our head, it must enter our feet, the lowest level. Our feet are creatures of habit; the daily routine of our lives must be filled with Torah. When we rejoice and dance we are joining the entire body, from the feet upward, with the Torah. When the lower levels are filled with Torah, the rest of the body follows, as it is written, I have thought about my ways, but my feet bring me back to Your Torah. (*Tehillim* 119:59)

❖

*A*nd you shall love Hashem your Lord with all your heart, all your spirit and all your possessions. And these words, which I command you today, shall be on your heart; and you shall study them . . . (*Devarim* 6:5)

These verses symbolize the fall holidays: "With all your heart" symbolizes *Rosh Hashanah*, the day of judgment, when we dedicate the heart to Hashem; "with all your spirit" represents *Yom Kippur*, which is a day when our spirit is withheld sustenance; "with all your possessions" is *Sukkos*, when we gather our produce from the fields and abandon our homes to sit in a temporary dwelling.

If one participates in those three holidays, then one is worthy of "and these words which I command you today shall be on your heart." This is the celebration of Torah on *Shemini Atzeress*.

———————— ❖ ————————

*T*he Kabbalists divide the year into two parts. The winter months are the potential, while the summer months are for revelation of the potential through activity. *Pesach* and *Shavuos* in the summer months correspond to *Sukkos* and *Shemini Atzeress* in the winter months.

The holiday of *Shavuos* commemorates the day we received the Ten Commandments, and it is called *Atzeress*, solemn assembly. The eighth day of *Sukkos*, is also called *Atzeress*, and we celebrate and rejoice with the Torah. The fruit that started growing on *Shavuos* has ripened.

———————— ❖ ————————

*T*he Torah contains a full account of the offerings, the libations and other holiday observances in the Beis Hamikdash. We no longer have many of them because the Beis Hamikdash was destroyed. Therefore, our celebration during the *Sukkos* holiday is concluded with a celebration of Torah, which connects us to the fullness of the holiday.

———————— ❖ ————————

*I*n the shadow of His shelter, I yearned to be; and His fruit was sweet to my palate. (*Shir Hashirim* 2:3) "His shelter" are the days of *Sukkos*. "His fruit is sweet" is the eighth day when we rejoice with the Torah.

❖

*F*rom the mouths of babes, you established strength to put to rest the enemy and the avenger. Who is man that You should remember him, and son of man that You should look after him? And You have made him slightly less than the Divine, and crowned him with honor, and You have let him rule over Your handiwork, all You have placed under his feet. (*Tehillim* 8:3-7)

These verses refer to the fall holidays. "Who is man that You should remember him" refers to the day of judgment of *Rosh Hashanah*.

"You made him slightly less than the Divine" refers to *Yom Kippur* when all the Jewish people purify themselves and are likened to angels.

"You have crowned him with honor" refers to *Sukkos*, when Hashem surrounded the Jewish nation with clouds of glory.

"You made him rule over your handiwork" refers to *Shemini Atzeress* of which it is written, A day of solemn assembly it should be for you; it is in your hands and your power.

The *Midrash* relates that when Hashem was about to give the Torah the angels complained, "Who is man that you should remember him?" Yet with effort, man can be slightly less than the Divine.

The Torah was offered to the other nations of the world before it was given to Klal Yisrael. The descendants of Esav refused it, because it forbade killing. The children of

151

Yishmael also refused it, because it forbade stealing. Yishmael was the son of Avraham who symbolized kindness, the right hand. Esav was the son of Yitzchak who symbolized strict judgment, the left hand. Today, Yishmael attempts to usurp the role of the Jewish people by outdoing their right hand by doing acts of kindness. Esav tries to usurp the role of the Jewish people by outdoing the left hand through acts of strict judgment.

However, the Torah is more powerful than these opposing hands, as it is written, The strength of His deeds He has related to His people. (*Tehillim* 111:6) This means that through the Torah we regain the strength originally intended for us. When we are connected to the roots of our being, the Torah, then we regain the use of both our hands. On the eighth day, *Shemini Atzeress*, the day of gathering, we gather energies that have gone astray.

The Torah is the inheritance of the children of Yaakov, whose energy is in his voice, as it is written, The voice is the voice of Yaakov, but the hands are the hands of Esav. (*Bereishis* 27:22) The voice of Yaakov is poised in balance with the hands of Esav, and on the eighth day, the balance tips. This is a foretaste of the time of *Mashiach* when Yaakov's voice is dominant over all the hands of all the nations of the earth.

❖

*I*t is written, Blessed is he who trusts in Hashem, and Hashem will be trustworthy to him. (*Yirmiyahu* 17:7)

Each item of creation appears as material reality. Yet, its true divine essence is concealed.

We can relate to the illusion or to the true reality. If we relate to the illusion and ignore the divine essence, we create an idol, a power independent of Hashem. If we relate to the true nature of the world, the divine, we give it existence and life; and we receive life in return.

Torah is life. It is written, And you who are connected to Hashem are alive. (*Devarim* 4:4) Therefore, whoever is connected to the Torah actually is connecting himself to the life within it.

On the eighth day, our trust in Hashem, which started growing on *Rosh Hashanah*, reaches maturity. Our connection with the Torah is at its peak. Let us rejoice in Hashem, with life, and the Torah, for the light and length of our days.

❖

A man came to Hillel and said, "Teach me the entire Torah while I stand on one foot." Hillel replied, "Do not unto others what you do not want done to you. This is the whole Torah; the rest is an explanation." (*Shabbos* 31a)

The entire Torah is summarized in the commandment, Love your neighbor as your own self. (*Vayikra* 19:18) The whole Torah is a prescription to produce one singularity from all the many parts. Therefore, the commandments are an explanation; each one makes clearer how the singularity is to be accomplished.

Similarly, the eighth day is a day to accomplish singularity, as it is written, On the eighth day, you shall have a solemn assembly. (*Bamidbar* 29:35) When we assemble all our energies, we are moving in the direction of Torah. Let us rejoice with the Torah and our good fortune of uniting with our people.

❖

*O*n the eighth day, we pray for rain, and we celebrate with the Torah. The rain helps crops grow. It produces fruits, but it also produces husks around the fruit. Fruit provides food necessary to sustain life, but it also contains impurities which cannot be absorbed by the body. This is the natural way of receiving gifts from Heaven.

The food of the Jews who wandered in the desert on their way out of Egypt, the manna, was different. Every part of it was absorbed by the body. There were no impurities in the food or in the bodies that absorbed it. The manna had no husk. It was not limited by a surrounding impurity; therefore, it was infinite. The strength we receive from the Torah is equally pure.

❖

*L*et us rejoice and be glad with the Torah for it is our strength and light. (*Yom Tov Tefillos*)

The Torah is a clear and infinite light. It is written, The *mitzvah* is a lamp and the Torah is the flame. (*Mishlei* 6:23) In order to have Torah, one must be prepared by performing the *mitzvos*. If not, the flame is left hanging in the air, and it is soon extinguished.

As a nation, we understood this when Moshe asked us whether or not we would accept the Torah. We answered, "We will do and we will listen." (*Shemos* 19:8) We realized that the only way we can have the light of the Torah is if we do first. That will give us the lamp to which to attach the flame of Torah.

At the beginning of the Jewish year, we prepare a lamp of *mitzvos*. The surge of extra *mitzvos* begins with the *mitzvah* of shofar on *Rosh Hashanah*. It continues with *Sukkos*, and its *sukkah*, *esrog*, *lulav*, *haddasim* and *aravos*. And it culminates in *Shemini Atzeress*, when the light of the Torah can be joined to this lamp.

If a person learns from his friend one chapter, even one

law, even one letter, he is to treat that friend with honor. (*Avos* 6:3) How much more must one honor the Torah itself, which teaches us how to serve Hashem! How do we honor the Torah? By studying it day and night, as it is written, If you seek her, it will elevate you. (*Mishlei* 4:8) Seek her as a poor person who gleans the fallen stalks of wheat after the reaping is done.

The Torah is infinite in its meaning. Each verse, word and letter contains limitless teachings and is connected to celestial worlds. We can only grasp at its fallen stalks. If we bend down to lift the stalks, we are uplifted in return.

When the Jewish people were ready to accept the Torah, they stood at the foot of the mountain. (*Shemos* 19:17) They felt worthy of the lowest part of Torah, but this humility elevated them to receive a much higher level of Torah.

The Torah is divine, neither fragmented nor made up of parts, and it is the Name of Hashem. It is written, Hashem wanted to benefit His righteous, that the Torah be magnified and strong. (*Yeshayahu* 42:21) He wanted to make the Jewish people worthy. Therefore, He gave them Torah and *mitzvos*. (*Makkos* 23b) This means that Hashem formed His holy Name in many different ways. His people can learn and live it—through picking up every detail of the Torah.

14

AND THIS IS THE BLESSING

On the last day, Simchas Torah, we read the last portion in the Torah, Parshas Vezos Habrachah, "this is the blessing." It is read with a special tune, followed by the reading of the very first portion of the Torah, Bereishis, "in the beginning."

Hashem has come from Mount Sinai and was shining forth from Seir. (*Devarim* 33:1) Hashem took the Torah to all the nations of the world to see if they would accept it. They did not; however, the Jewish nation finally did accept it. The *Zohar* states that the nations refusal generated a more powerful light than we were to have received.

The Torah has many levels of meaning. If it were given to the angels, it would have been understood on a far less physical level. If it would have been given to the descendants of Esav and Yishmael, it would have had a much more physical meaning. Therefore, when the nations refused the Torah, we received their meanings too. This is why the Torah starts with the story of Creation, so that we can understand the Torah even on the level of nature and physical events.

———————— ❖ ————————

*F*rom His right Hand came the fire of Law. (*Devarim* 33:1)

The Torah is a fire which could consume those who come near it. It is above human understanding, and it is only by the mercy of Hashem that we can learn it. Thus, when Moshe wandered onto the mountain of Hashem, and "behold the bush is burning, but it is not consumed." (*Shemos* 3:2) Therefore, even those who are not consumed by the fire and fervor can still benefit from the Torah by being part of the burning bush of Klal Yisrael.

———————— ❖ ————————

*T*he Torah was commanded to us by Moshe; an inheritance to the congregation of Yaakov. (*Devarim* 33:4)

The Jewish people at Mount Sinai asked Moshe to transmit the Torah to them saying, "Let not the Lord speak to us lest we die." (*Shemos* 20:19) They knew that if Hashem spoke directly to them, it would not last forever. Nothing can preserve the intensity of the Mount Sinai revelation. The reason the congregation of Yaakov has the Torah as a permanent heritage is because the Torah was commanded to us by Moshe. The human transmission of Torah is possible to preserve.

———————— ❖ ————————

A nd this is the blessing that Moshe blessed . . . (*Devarim* 33:1)

If one is leading the blessings with the congregation and makes a mistake, another person should continue from where the first one had stopped. (*Midrash Rabbah, Devarim*) Moshe, too, started where Yaakov had stopped.

The Jewish people are ready to receive Hashem's blessing. Even if there are evildoers among them, there is always someone who can restore them to righteousness. The true blessing of Israel is that when one great leader is gone, there is another to replace him. Where Yaakov's blessings end is where the blessings of Moshe begin.

H e also loves the nations, all the holy ones are in Your Hand, and they press themselves to Your Feet and they follow Your Word. (*Devarim* 33:3)

There are four kinds of existence: inanimate objects, growing plants, animals and man, and above all of them—the chosen people. To reach the fullness of one existence, one must bring the lower levels closer to their divine purpose. Man must first connect all the lower levels to their proper roots if he is to be complete. Therefore, the Jewish people bring offerings for all the seventy nations in order that they will be able to come to their level.

A nd they press themselves to Your Feet. (*Devarim* 33:3)

The Jews were miraculously saved from the slavery of Egypt, and Hashem was ready to present them with the Torah. However, they started to have feelings of pride. Therefore, Hashem took them through the desert for seven weeks. When they regained their humility they were ready for the Torah.

After *Rosh Hashanah* and *Yom Kippur*, we are free from slavery to our evil desires. But there is an inclination to arrogance; therefore, we are asked to leave our comfortable homes and to enter the *sukkah*. We regain our humility; and after seven days, we are able to rejoice with the Torah. To the degree that one humbles himself to the feet of Hashem one can acquire a share of Torah. The *Zohar* states that if one is like the doorstep, constantly trodden, then the *Shechinah*, Divine Presence, lifts him up to great heights. (*Zohar, Devarim*)

---------- ❖ ----------

*A*nd Hashem came from Sinai, and shone forth from Seir, came forth from Paran, and with Him multitudes of angels. (*Devarim* 33:2)

There are four levels of learning Torah: the simple explanation—*pshat*; the hinted allusion—*remez*; the exegesis—*drush*; and the hidden meaning—*sod*. The first three are constantly threatened by evil. Sinai also means hatred, for the arrogant nations hated the Jews after they received the Torah. Seir are the descendants of Esav, and Paran are the children of Yishmael, two nations that constantly threaten the Torah. Only the secret and hidden learning is never threatened. No one can touch that, for this is the realm of the multitude of angels.

Similarly, the three holidays, *Pesach, Shavuos* and *Sukkos* each correspond to one of the forefathers—Avraham, Yitzchak and Yaakov. Each of those had been threatened, but *Shemini Atzeress* represents David Hamelech, the one who will bring the complete redemption.

*A*ll the holy ones are in Your Hand; and they press themselves to Your Feet and they follow Your Word. (*Devarim* 33:3)

The Jewish people are the witnesses that Hashem is the Master of the World. It is written, "You are my witnesses," says the Lord. (*Yeshayahu* 43:12) Since a relative is not allowed to be a witness, how can the Jews serve as witnesses, for they are as close to Hashem as children to their father? The truth is that the Jewish people do not pronounce testimony. Though they live according to a high standard of social morality, they humble themselves as the lowest of people. When people see the humility of the Jewish people, they realize that the world has a Master. When people see that the Jews are pressed to the Feet of Hashem, the nations realize that the Jews follow His Word. Thus, the nations also become believers in Hashem.

---

*A*nd there was a king among the Jewish nation. (*Devarim* 33:5) King means the Torah, and it also means Moshe. How are these two interpretations reconciled?

Moshe gave us the Torah, and Hashem promised us the services of Moshe for the teaching of the Torah. Therefore, each time people gather to study Torah, the teaching energy of Moshe is evident.

Furthermore, the Torah is composed of the Names of Hashem, which are the twenty-two letters of the Hebrew alphabet. The Names of Hashem are like royal robes; they enhance the splendor of the king in the eyes of his subjects each time they are worn. The study of the Torah is the display of these royal robes. The teaching of Moshe, evident each time Torah is learned, enables us to appreciate the King of Kings. Moshe, and through him the Torah, the kings, allows us to draw nearer to the King of Kings.

———————— ❖ ————————

A nd this is the blessing with which Moshe blessed the Jewish people . . . (*Devarim* 33:1)

We recite a blessing before reading the Torah scroll and after we finish. We can compare this to the blessing we make before and after we eat. Before eating, we thank Hashem that He is providing food for our hunger. After eating, we thank Him for the vitality and energy that we have obtained from the food.

Two holidays celebrate the giving of the Torah. On *Shavuos* we rejoice before receiving the Torah, grateful that Hashem satisfied our spiritual hunger. On *Shemini Atzeress*, the eighth day, we rejoice in the privilege of absorbing the Torah.

In the blessing after the Torah reading we say, "And everlasting life He has planted in us." We were granted the energy to add new interpretations, the Oral Law, and this power and insight was also given by Moshe. He planted the *Torah Shebe'al Peh* inside us. Therefore, it is written, And this is the blessing that Moshe blessed . . . This is the blessing after the Torah, for the absorption of the Torah deep in our bones, for the Oral Torah that each one of us innovates.

———————— ❖ ————————

T he blessing after the Torah reading notes "that He gave us a teaching of truth." (*Tefillas Shacharis*).

The Torah reveals the divine truth in the world, which is full of lies and illusion. The Torah reveals the divine nature of every existing thing. All truth has Torah as its foundation.

161

Similarly, the inner nature of man is revealed when he is connected to the Torah. Therefore, we say, "The Torah was commanded to us by Moshe—*Torah tzivah lonu Moshe*." The first Hebrew letters spell *tzelem*, image. The Torah reveals the Image of Hashem in man.

❖

*T*he Torah was commanded to us by Moshe; an inheritance for the children of Yaakov. (*Devarim* 33:4)

Avraham, Yitzchak and Yaakov lived a Torah life long before the Mount Sinai revelation, because they inherently perceived Hashem's Hand in every aspect of the world. We inherit some of this sensitivity from our ancestors, as we say in the blessing over the Torah, "He planted in us an everlasting life." The *Torah Shebiksav* is the key to open the hearts of the Jewish people to find the treasure within each Jew. The Oral Law, the *Torah Shebe'al Peh* grows out of one's own being. The revelation at Mount Sinai gave us keys for the inner heritage within our hearts.

❖

*A*nd all of the strong hand that Moshe had displayed before the eyes of the Jewish nation. (*Devarim* 34:12) It is also written, In the beginning Hashem created the heavens and the earth . . . (*Bereishis* 1:1)

The creation of the world was for the revelation of its divine nature. This revelation was constant during the years the Jews wandered in the desert. This was the strong hand that Moshe displayed, it showed them the essence of all existence.

❖

And this is the blessing which Moshe blessed . . . (*Devarim* 33:1) In the beginning when Hashem created the Heavens and the earth . . . (*Bereishis* 1:1)

Why does the creation of the world start with a *beis*, the second letter of the Hebrew alphabet? Why not the *alef*, the first letter? *Alef* can spell *arur*, cursed; and the Creation (Torah) is a blessing. Moreover, *beis* can spell *brachah*, blessing; Hashem looked at the world and blessed it, saying, "May it last!" (*Midrash Rabbah, Bereishis* 1:1)

The Torah that was presented at Mount Sinai starts with an *alef–anochi*, I am. There is no fear of *arur*, curse, because Torah is the root of blessing. It transforms even the curse into a blessing. The path of the righteous ends up as a smooth road, even if it starts with thorns.

Even the curses mentioned in the Torah can be turned into blessings for those bound closely to the Torah. The existence of evil is also a kindness of Hashem. Whoever is receptive to the inner nature of the universe, receives the curses as a blessing even on a material level.

And this is the blessing . . . The Torah starts with concealed blessing and ends with open blessing. Those who are worthy can immediately proceed to the full blessing.

❖

The Torah was commanded to us by Moshe . . . (*Devarim* 33:4)

The souls of the Jewish people are the lamps on which the flame of the Torah can rest. It is written, The *mitzvah* is a lamp and the Torah is the flame. (*Mishlei* 6:23) And it is also written, Man's soul is the lamp of Hashem. (*Mishlei* 20:27)

Some generations have better lamps for Torah, while others have pitifully poor ones. Then the Torah is in exile, for it is written, I am (*anochi*) with him in [his time of] sorrow. (*Tehillim* 91:15) When the Jewish people are in trouble, then the *anochi* of the first of the Ten Commandments is also in trouble.

— ❖ —

A nd all the firm hand . . . which Moshe did before the eyes of all the Jewish nation (*Devarim* 34:12) In the beginning . . . (*Bereishis* 1:1)

Moshe performed all his miracles with the energy of the beginning, which is the Torah, the root of the entire universe. Likewise, every item of Creation can be restored to its proper place with Torah energy. If the world can be created with the Torah, surely it can be fixed with it.

— ❖ —

A nd this is . . . (*vezos*)

The eighth day of *Sukkos* is connected to the eighth day of *Chanukah*, which is called *Zos Chanukah*. Both days are the culmination of their respective holidays. They are on the level of eight, totally beyond nature and reaching into the World-to-Come.

APPENDIX

❖

GLOSSARY
REFERENCES

GLOSSARY

❖

alef: Hebrew letter
aravah (aravos): willow branch(es)
arba minim: four species taken on *Sukkos*
Avraham: Abraham
baal (baalei) teshuvah: penitent(s)
Bamidbar: Book of Numbers
Beis Hamikdash: Holy Temple in Jerusalem
Bereishis: Book of Genesis
brachah: blessing
chaf: Hebrew letter
Chag Haassif: Harvest Festival
Chanukah: Festival of Lights
chassidism: Jewish pietist movement
chukim: statutes
chuppah: bridal canopy
daled: Hebrew letter
derech eretz: common decency
Devarim: Book of Deuteronomy
drush: homiletics
Eichah: Book of Lamentations
Eretz Yisrael: Israel
Esav: Esau

esrog(im): citron, one of the four species taken on *Sukkos*
Ezras Nashim: women's section
galus: exile
Gemara: part of the Talmud
geshem: rain
haddas(im): myrtle branch(es), one of the four species taken on *Sukkos*
Hallel: special prayer of praise
Hashem: the Name, G-d
hashgachah pratis: specific providence
hay: Hebrew letter
hergel: habit
Hoshanna Rabbah: part of *Sukkos*
Hoshaya: Book of Hosea
Iyov: Book of Job
Kabbalah: mystical teachings
Kesuvim: Book of Hagiographa
Kiseh Hakavod: Throne of Glory
Klal Yisrael: the Jewish people
Kodesh Kadashim: Holy of Holies
kohein (kohanim): hereditary priest(s)
kohein gadol: high priest
Koheles: Book of Ecclesiastes
lug: liquid measurement
lulav: palm frond, one of the four species taken on *Sukkos*
Maariv: evening prayers
Mashiach: the Messiah
matanah: present
matzah (matzos): unleavened bread(s)
Melachim: Book of Kings
meorasah: betrothed
mezuzah: scroll affixed to the doorpost
midbar: desert
mikveh: ritual bath
Mishkan: Tabernacle
Mishlei: Book of Proverbs
Mishnah: part of the Talmud

mishpatim: laws
mitzvah (mitzvos): Torah commandment(s)
morashah: heritage
Moshe: Moses
nachal: brook
nefesh: spirit
netzach: eternity
Neviim: prophets
ohel: tent
olam: world
Olam Haba: the World-to-Come
Pesach: Passover, early spring festival
pshat: simple meaning
rasha: villain
remez: allusion
Rosh Hashanah: New Year; tractate of the Talmud
Sanhedrin: tractate of the Talmud
Shabbos: the Sabbath; tractate of the Talmud
Shacharis: morning prayers
Shavuos: Pentecost, late spring festival
Shechinah: Divine Presence
Shemini Atzeress: Festival of the Eighth Day
Shemoneh Esrei: the Eighteen Benedictions, fundamental part of daily prayers
Shemos: Book of Exodus
Shir Hashirim: Song of Songs
Shlomo: Solomon
Shmuel: Book of Samuel
shofar: ram's horn
shtei halachem:
Simchas Torah: Festival of the Torah
sukkah (sukkos): Sukkos booths
Sukkos: Festival of Tabernacles, autumn festival
Talmud: the Oral law
talmid chacham: Torah scholars
tefillin: phylacteries
Tehillim: Book of Psalms

tekiah: type of *shofar* sound
teruah: type of *shofar* sound
teshuvah: repentance, responsum
Torah: the complete body of Jewish teachings
tzaddik(im): righteous person (people)
tzelem: image
vav: Hebrew letter
Vayikra: Book of Leviticus
Yaakov: Jacob
yad: hand
Yamim Noraim: festivals
Yechezkel: Book of Ezekiel
Yerushalayim: Jerusalem
Yeshayahu: Book of Isaiah
Yirmiyahu: Book of Jeremiah
Yishmael: Ishmael
Yisrael: Israel
Yitzchak: Isaac
Yom Kippur: Day of Atonement
Yosef: Joseph
yud: Hebrew letter
zatzal: short for *zecher tzaddik livrachah*
Zechariah: Book of Zacharias
zecher tzaddik livrachah: the memory of a righteous person is a
blessing
zera: offspring
Zohar: fundamental Kabbalistic tract

REFERENCES

❖

The following is a list of sources for each chapter of the book. Because of the particular organization of the *sefarim* of the Sfas Emes, it seemed more practical to give the sources according to page number. The page numbers listed for each chapter follow the sequence of selections as they appear in the edition published by Yahadus (Bnei Brak, Israel, 1971, Volume Five), one of the more popular current editions.

1. The Time of Our Rejoicing
    200, 204, 230, 232, 231, 237, 195, 199, 194

2. That Your Generations Shall Know
    181, 187, 181, 181, 181, 187, 198, 198, 187, 190, 206, 218, 205, 223, 217

3. Clouds of Glory
    230, 202, 214, 218, 221, 225, 230

4. The Kindness of Youth
    187, 188, 194, 230, 224, 225, 229, 230, 236